Introduction to Our New S...

The Science Coordination Group was set up with the aim of prod... material for National Curriculum Science. Following popular demand we have taken our very successful Revision Guides for GCSE double science and from them produced a number of syllabus-specific versions for the NEAB and SEG double science syllabuses.

All of our Revision Guides exhibit several crucial features which set them apart from the rest:

1) Careful and Complete Explanations

Unlike other revision guides, we do not restrict ourselves to a brief outline of the bare essentials. Instead we work hard to give complete, concise and carefully written details on each topic.

2) Deliberate Use of Humour and Colourful Language

We consider the humour to be an essential part of our Revision Guides. It is there to keep the reader interested and entertained, and we are certain that it greatly assists their learning.
(It is not however expected to win us any awards...)

3) Carefully Matched to the SEG Coordinated Syllabus, and more...

We have taken great care to ensure that this book follows the exact detail of the SEG double award coordinated syllabus.
Once again however we feel that merely illustrating the syllabus is an inadequate approach.
We have therefore done rather more than simply list the basic syllabus details and add pictures.
Instead we have endeavoured to include all the relevant explanation which appears to us to be necessary. The result is a full 92 pages giving a clear explanation of the whole syllabus content.
We hope that you will appreciate the amount of time and care which has gone into this.

This book is suitable for both Higher and Foundation Tier candidates.
The material which is required only for higher tier is clearly indicated in blue boxes like this.
In addition, the Higher Tier questions in the Revision Summaries are printed in blue.

And Keep Learning the Basic Facts...

Throughout these books there is constant emphasis on the inescapable need to keep learning the basic facts. This simple message is hammered home without compromise and without remorse, and whilst this traditionally brutal philosophy may not be quite in line with some other approaches to education, we still rather like it. But only because it works.

Contents

Section One — Electricity and Magnetism

(1.1) *Electric charge* .... Static Electricity 1
" " .... Current and Charge 3
(1.2) *Energy in circuits* .... Circuits 4
" " " .... Series Circuits 6
" " " .... Parallel Circuits 8
" " " .... Energy in Circuits 10
(1.4) *Electromagnetic forces* .... Magnetic Fields 11
" " .... Electromagnets 12
" " .... The Electric Motor 13
(1.5) *Electromagnetic induction* .... Electromagnetic Induction 14
(1.6) *Transformers* .... Transformers 16
" .... The National Grid 17
(1.7) *Mains electricity / (1.3) Power* .... Electricity in the Home 18
Revision Summary for Section One 20

Section Two — Forces and Motion

(2.1) *Speed and velocity* .... Speed and Velocity 21
(2.2) *Force and acceleration* .... Forces and Acceleration 22
" " " .... Laws of Motion 23
" " " .... Resultant Forces 24
" " " .... Reaction Forces and Friction 25
" " " .... Stopping Distances for Cars 26
(2.3) *Force and non-uniform motion* .... Mass, Weight and Gravity 27
" " " " .... Terminal Velocity 28
(2.4) *Force and pressure on solids, etc.* .... Turning Forces 29
" " " " " " .... Hooke's Law 30
" " " " " " .... Pressure on Surfaces 31
" " " " " " .... Pressure = Force / Area 32
" " " " " " .... Pressure in Gases 33
Revision Summary for Section Two 34

Section Three — Waves

(3.1) *Characteristics of waves* .... Basic Principles 35
" " " .... The Wave Equation 36
(3.2) *Light* .... Reflection 37
" .... Refraction 38
" .... Refraction: Two Special Cases 39
" .... Total Internal Reflection 40
" .... Diffraction 41
(3.3) *The electromagnetic spectrum* .... The E.M. Spectrum 42
" " " .... Microwaves and Infrared 43
" " " .... Visible, UV, X-rays, γ-Rays 44
(3.4) *Sound* .... Sound Waves 45
" .... Ultrasound 47
" .... The Speed of Sound 48
" .... Seismic Waves 49
Revision Summary for Section Three 50

(SEG Syllabus reference)

Section Four — The Earth and Beyond

(4.1) *The solar system*
- The Solar System 51
- The Planets 52
- Moons, Asteroids and Comets 53
- The Cause of Days and Seasons 54
- Satellites 55

(4.2) *The wider Universe*
- The Universe 56

(4.3) *Evolution of the Universe and stars*
- The Origin of the Universe 57
- The Life Cycle of Stars 58
- Revision Summary for Section Four 59

Section Five — Energy Resources & Energy Transfer

(5.1) *Energy resources*
- Sources of Power 60
- Power from Non-Renewables 61
- Power from Renewables 62

(5.2) *Energy transfers*
- Types of Energy Transfer 64
- Heat Transfer 65
- Conduction of Heat 66
- Convection of Heat 67
- Heat Radiation 68
- Heat Transfer Summary 69
- Applications of Heat Transfer 70
- Useful Energy Transfers 71
- Efficiency of Machines 72
- Energy Conservation 73

(5.3) *Work, power and energy*
- Work Done, Energy and Power 74
- Kinetic and Potential Energy 75
- K.E. and P.E. — Some Examples 76
- Revision Summary for Section Five 77

Section Six — Radioactivity

(6.1) *Characteristics and detection*
- Atomic Structure 78
- Types of Radiation 79
- Background Radiation 81
- Half-life 82
- Half-life Calculations 83

(6.2) *Effects and uses*
- Radiation and the Body 84
- Uses of Radioactive Materials 85
- Revision Summary for Section Six 86

(SEG Syllabus reference)

Answers 86

Index 87

Published by Coordination Group Publications
Typesetting and Layout by The Science Coordination Group
Illustrations by: Sandy Gardner e-mail: zimkit@aol.com

Consultant Editor: Paddy Gannon BSc MA

Text, design, layout and illustrations © Richard Parsons 1998.   All rights reserved.
With thanks to CorelDRAW for providing one or two jolly bits of clipart.

Printed by Hindson Print, Newcastle upon Tyne.

ELECTRICITY AND MAGNETISM

Static Electricity — Electric Charge

Static electricity is all about charges that are *NOT* free to move. This causes them to build up in one place and it often ends with a *spark* or a *shock* when they do finally move.

1) Build-Up of Static Is Caused by Friction

1) When two *insulating* materials are *rubbed* together, electrons will be *scraped off one* and *dumped* on the other.
2) This'll leave a *positive* static charge on one and a *negative* static charge on the other.
3) *Which way* the electrons are transferred *depends* on the *two materials* involved.
4) Electrically charged objects *attract* small objects placed near them.
   (Try this: rub a balloon on a woolly pully — then put it near tiddly bits of paper and watch them jump.)
5) The classic examples are *polythene* and *acetate* rods being rubbed with a *cloth duster*, as shown in the diagrams:

With the *polythene rod*, electrons move *from the duster* to the rod.

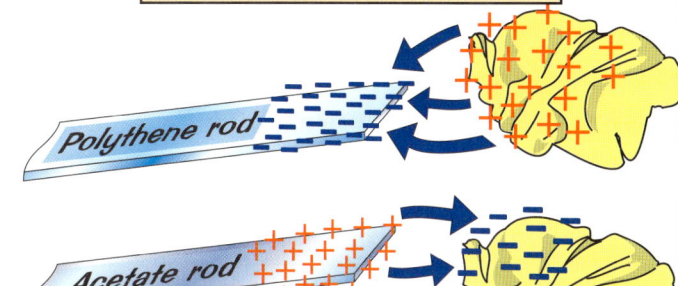

With the *acetate rod*, electrons move *from the rod* to the duster.

2) Only Electrons Move — Never the Positive Charges

Watch out for this in Exams. Both +ve and −ve electrostatic charges are only ever produced by the movement of *electrons*. The positive charges *definitely do not move*! A positive static charge is always caused by electrons *moving* away elsewhere, as shown above. Don't forget!

A charged conductor can be *discharged safely* by connecting it to earth with a *metal strap*. The electrons flow *down* the strap to the ground if the charge is *negative* and flow *up* the strap from the ground if the charge is *positive*.

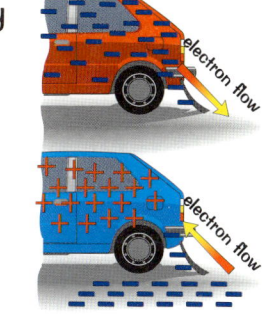

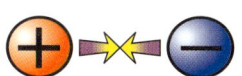

3) Like Charges Repel, Opposite Charges Attract

This is *easy* and, I'd have thought, *kind of obvious*.
Two things with *opposite* electric charges are *attracted* to each other.
Two things with the *same* electric charge will *repel* each other.
These forces get *weaker* the *further apart* the two things are.

4) Sparks Are Caused by Unbalanced Charges

The greater the *CHARGE* on an *isolated* object, the greater the *VOLTAGE* between it and the earth. If the voltage gets *big enough* there's a *spark* which *jumps* across the gap. High voltage cables can be *dangerous* for this reason. Big sparks have been known to *leap* from *overhead cables* to earth. But not often.

Phew — it's enough to make your hair stand on end...

The way to tackle this page is to first *learn the four headings* till you can *scribble them all down*. Then learn all the details, and keep practising by *covering the page* and scribbling down the headings with as many details as you can remember for each one. Just *keep trying*...

SECTION ONE — ELECTRICITY AND MAGNETISM   SEG SYLLABUS

Static Electricity

Electric Charge

They like asking you to give *quite detailed examples* in Exams. Make sure you *learn all these details*.

Static Electricity Being Helpful:

Dust Removal in Chimneys:

1) Just put a set of *charged plates* in a *chimney* or extractor duct and the particles of smoke or dust will be *attracted* to them.
2) Every now and then you *turn off* the electricity and *shake the dust into a bag* — easy peasy. These are known as *electrostatic smoke precipitators*.

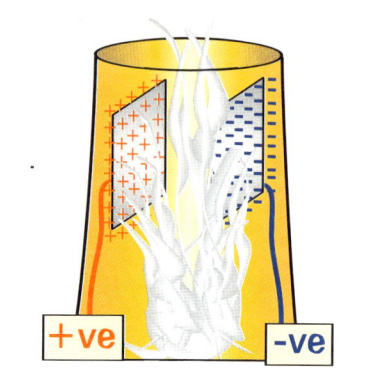

+ve   -ve

Static Electricity Being a Little Joker:

Clothing Crackles

When *synthetic clothes* are *dragged* over each other (like in a *tumble drier*) or over your *head*, electrons get scraped off, leaving *unbalanced charges* between the parts, and that leads to the inevitable: — *forces of attraction* (i.e. they stick together) and little *sparks/shocks* as the charges *rearrange themselves*.

Static Electricity Playing at Terrorist:

1) Lightning

Rain droplets fall to Earth with *positive charge*. This creates a *huge charge inbalance* and a *big spark*.

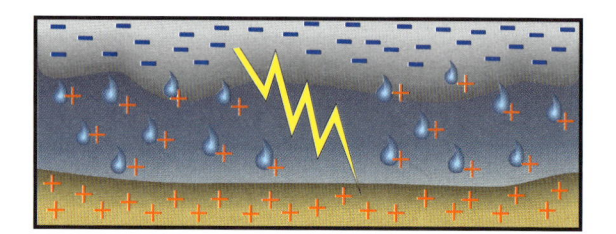

2) The Old Fuel-Filling Nightmare:

1) As *fuel* flows out of a *filler pipe*, static charge can *build up*.
2) This can easily lead to a *SPARK*, which can ignite the fuel vapour and — *BOOM!*
3) *The solution*: make the nozzles out of *METAL* so that the charge is *conducted away*, instead of building up.
4) It's also good to have *earthing straps* between the *fuel tank* and the *fuel pipe*.

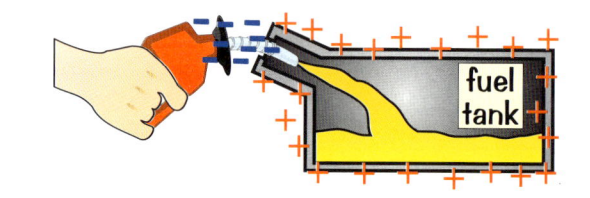

fuel tank

Static electricity — learn the shocking truth...

This page is nicely broken up into three main sections, which makes it quite a bit easier to learn. First learn the main headings, then the subheadings, and then all the details that go with each. Slowly you *build it all up* in your head till you can *scribble it all down*.

SEG SYLLABUS   SECTION ONE — ELECTRICITY AND MAGNETISM

Current and Charge

Electric Charge

Current Is Just the Flow of Charges

1) **CURRENT** flows any time *charge moves from one place to another*. Of course with a *spark* it doesn't last very long. But join up a few bits of wire in a loop and you've got a *circuit*. Give it a *power supply* — like a *battery* — and current can flow *continually* (...well, until your battery runs out).

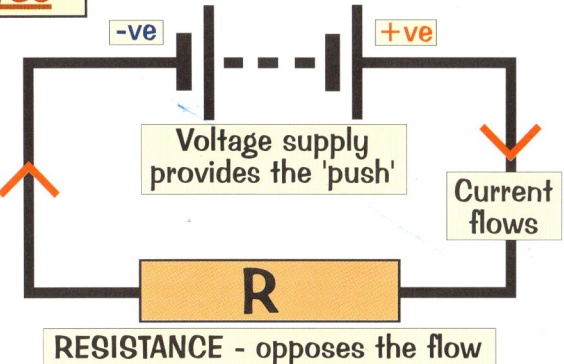

Charges Are Normally Electrons, but...

If the current is flowing through a **SOLUTION**, the charges are dissolved **IONS**.

Isn't electricity great... Mind you it's pretty bad news if the words don't mean anything to you — so why not *learn some now*. Here's the other essentials:

2) **VOLTAGE** is the *driving force* that pushes the current round. Kind of like *"electrical pressure"*.
3) **RESISTANCE** is anything in the circuit which *slows the flow down*.
4) **THERE'S A BALANCE**: the *voltage* is trying to *push* the current round the circuit, and the *resistance* is *opposing* it — the *relative sizes* of the voltage and resistance decide *how big* the current will be:

> If you *increase the VOLTAGE* — then **MORE CURRENT** will flow.
> If you *increase the RESISTANCE* — then **LESS CURRENT** will flow
> (or **MORE VOLTAGE** will be needed to keep the **SAME CURRENT** flowing).

It's Just Like the Flow of Water Around a Set of Pipes

1) The *current* is simply like the *flow of water*.
2) The *voltage* is like the *pressure* provided by a *pump* which pushes the stuff round.
3) *Resistance* is any sort of *constriction* in the flow, which is what the pressure has to *work against*.
4) If you *turn up the pump* and provide more *pressure* (or *"voltage"*), the flow will *increase*.
5) If you put in more *constrictions* (*"resistance"*), the flow (current) will *decrease*.

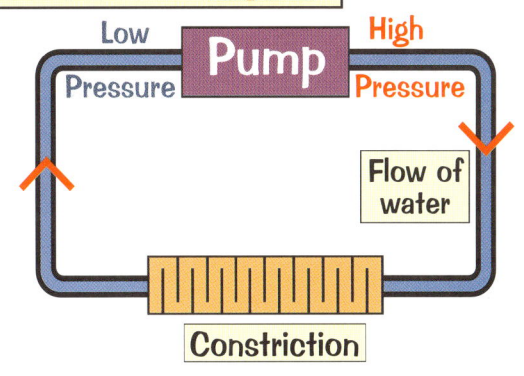

Charge Is Measured in Coulombs — Given by the Formula "Q=It"

When *current* (I) flows past a point in a circuit for a length of *time* (t) then *charge* (Q) has passed. This is given by the formula: $Q = It$

More charge passes around the circuit when a *bigger current* flows.

EXAMPLE: A charge of 15 coulombs flows past a point in 3 seconds. What is the current?
ANSWER: I = Q/t = 15/3 = 5A.

Understanding circuits — easy as pie...

This page is all about electric currents and what a circuit is, and how it works. This is the most basic stuff on electricity there is. I assume you realise that you'll never be able to learn anything else about electricity until you know this stuff... Good-oh. *Learn and scribble...*

SECTION ONE — ELECTRICITY AND MAGNETISM   SEG SYLLABUS

Circuits

Energy in Circuits

This is without doubt the most totally bog-standard circuit the world has ever known. So know it.

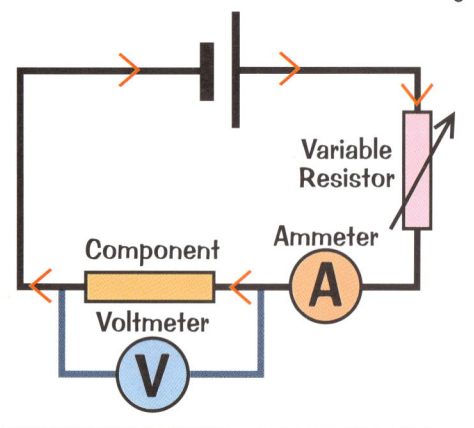

The Ammeter

1) Measures the _current_ (in _amps_) flowing through the component.
2) Must be placed _in series_.
3) Can be put _anywhere_ in series in the _main circuit_, but _never in parallel_ like the voltmeter.

The Voltmeter

1) Measures the _voltage_ (in _volts_) across the component.
2) Must be placed _in parallel_ around the _component under test_ — _NOT_ around the variable resistor or the battery!
3) The _proper_ name for "_voltage_" is "_potential difference_" or "_P.D._".

Five Important Points

1) This _very basic circuit_ is used for _testing components_, and for getting _V-I graphs_ for them.
2) The _component_, the _ammeter_ and the _variable resistor_ are all _in series_, which means they can be put _in any order_ in the main circuit. The _voltmeter_, on the other hand, can only be placed _in parallel_ around the _component under test_, as shown. Anywhere else is a definite _no-no_.
3) As you _vary_ the _variable resistor_ it alters the _current_ flowing through the circuit.
4) This allows you to take several **PAIRS OF READINGS** from the _ammeter_ and _voltmeter_.
5) You can then _plot_ these values for _current_ and _voltage_ on a _V-I graph_, like the ones below.

Four Hideously Important Voltage-Current Graphs

V-I graphs show how the current varies as you change the voltage. Learn these four real well:

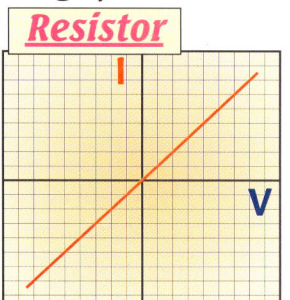

Resistor
The current through a **RESISTOR** (at constant temperature) is _proportional to voltage_.

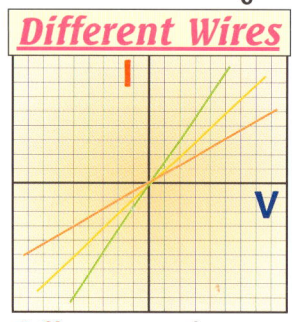

Different Wires
Different wires have different _resistances_, hence the different _slopes_.

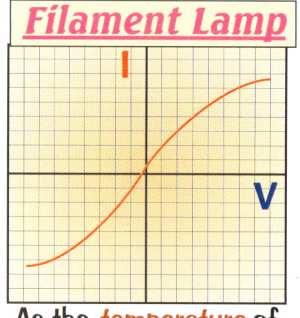

Filament Lamp
As the _temperature_ of the filament _increases_, the _resistance increases_, hence the _curve_.

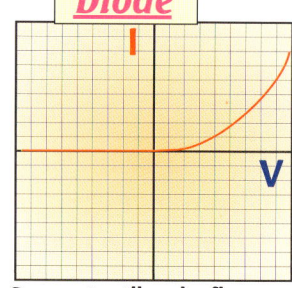

Diode
Current will only flow through a diode _in one direction_, as shown.

Calculating Resistance: $R = V/I$, (or R = "1/gradient")

Resistance is measured in _OHMS_, with the funny Greek symbol Ω (omega). For the _straight-line graphs_ the resistance of the component is _steady_ and is equal to the _inverse_ of the _gradient_ of the line, or "_1/gradient_". In other words the _STEEPER_ the graph, the _LOWER_ the resistance. If the graph _curves_, it means that the resistance is _changing_.
In that case R can be found for any point by taking the _pair of values_ (V,I) from the graph and sticking them in the formula $R = V/I$. Easy.

$$\text{Resistance} = \frac{\text{Potential Difference}}{\text{Current}}$$

In the end, you'll have to learn this — resistance is futile...

There are quite a lot of important details on this page and you need to _learn all of them_. The only way to make sure you really know it is to _cover up the page_ and see how much of it you can _scribble down_ from _memory_. Sure, it's not that easy — but it's the only way. Enjoy.

Circuits

Energy in Circuits

Circuit Symbols You Should Know:

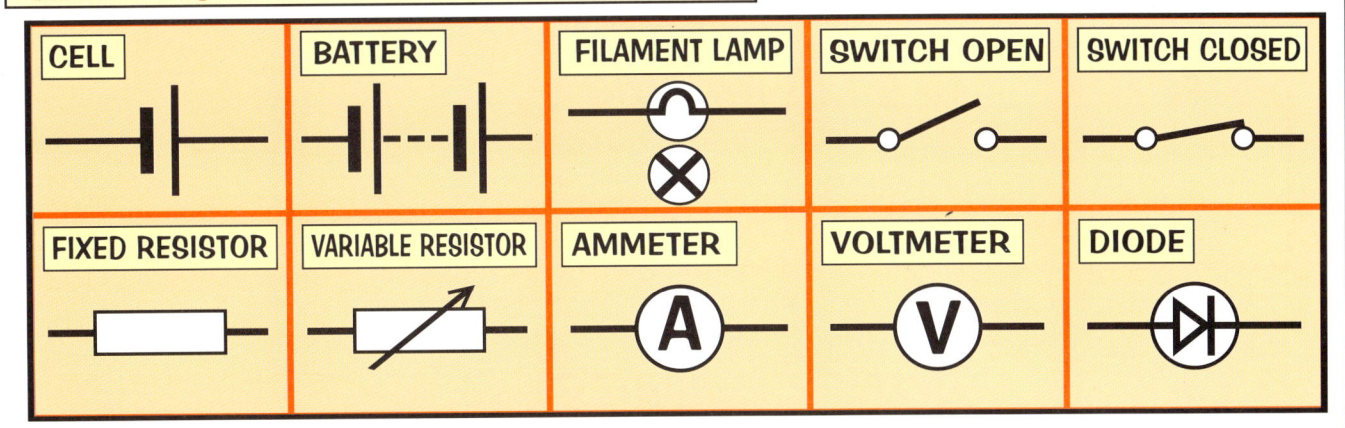

CELL	BATTERY	FILAMENT LAMP	SWITCH OPEN	SWITCH CLOSED
FIXED RESISTOR	VARIABLE RESISTOR	AMMETER	VOLTMETER	DIODE

2) Diode (or "Semiconductor Diode")

A special device made from *semiconductor* material such as *silicon*.
It lets current flow freely through it in *one direction*, but *not* in the other
(i.e. there's a very high resistance in the *reverse* direction).
This turns out to be real useful in various *electronic circuits*.

3) Light Dependent Resistor or "LDR" to You

1) In *bright light*, the resistance *falls*.
2) In *darkness*, the resistance is *highest*.
3) This makes it a useful device for various *electronic circuits* e.g. *automatic night lights*; *burglar detectors*.
4) At a given *light intensity*, the *voltage-current graph* will be a *straight line*, as with a *normal resistor*.

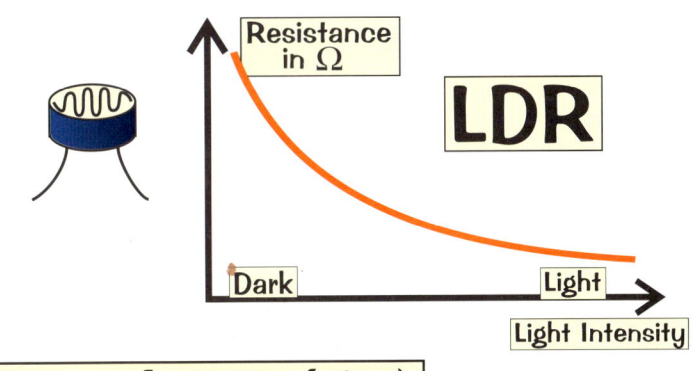

4) Thermistor (Temperature-Dependent Resistor)

1) In *hot* conditions, the resistance *drops*.
2) In *cool* conditions, the resistance goes *up*.
3) Thermistors make useful *temperature detectors*, e.g. *car engine* temperature sensors and electronic *thermostats*.
4) At a given *temperature*, the *voltage-current graph* will be a *straight line*, as with a *normal resistor*. However, because *current* produces a *heating effect*, in practice the greater the current, the less the resistance, so the *voltage-current graph* will *curve upwards*. So be careful.

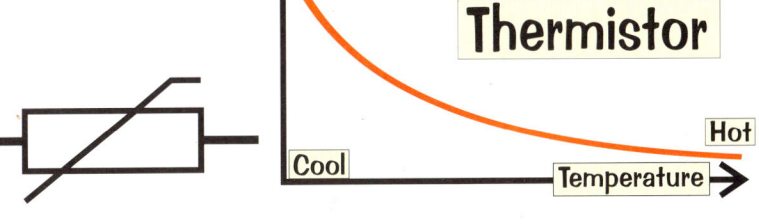

Higher Higher Higher

"Diode" — wasn't that a film starring Bruce Willis...

Another page of basic but important details about electrical circuits. You need to know all those circuit symbols as well as the extra details for the special devices below them. When you think you know it all try *covering the page* and *scribbling it all down*. See how you did, *then try again*.

SECTION ONE — ELECTRICITY AND MAGNETISM

SEG SYLLABUS

Series Circuits

Energy in Circuits

You need to be able to tell the difference between series and parallel circuits *just by looking at them*. You also need to know the *rules* about what happens with both types. Read on.

Series Circuits — All or Nothing

1) In *series circuits*, the different components are connected *in a line*, *end to end*, between the +ve and –ve of the power supply (except for *voltmeters*, which are always connected *in parallel*, but they don't count as part of the circuit).
2) If you remove or disconnect *one* component, the circuit is *broken* and they all *stop*.
3) This is generally *not very handy*, and in practice, *very few things* are connected in series.

1) Potential Difference Is Shared:

1) In series circuits the *total P.D.* of the *supply* is *shared* between the various *components*.
2) The *voltages* round a series circuit *always add up* to equal the *source voltage*:

$$V = V_1 + V_2$$

V = 1.5 + 1.5 = 3V

$$V = V_1 + V_2$$

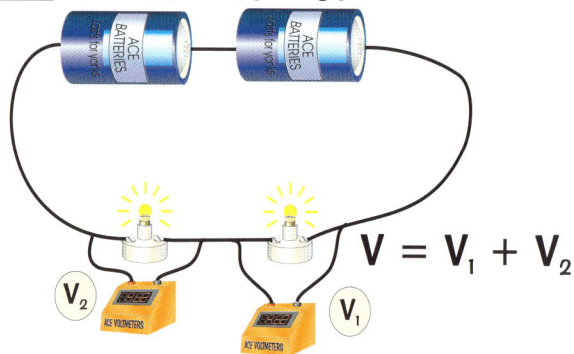

2) Current Is the Same Everywhere:

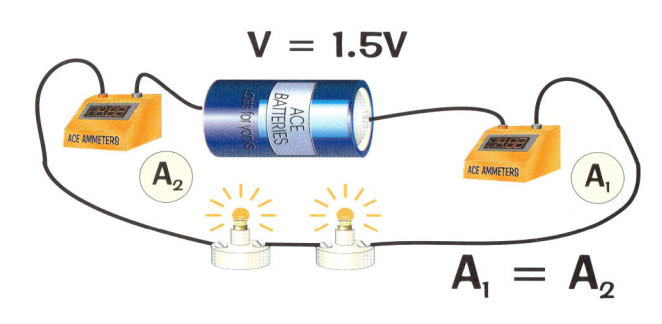

V = 1.5V

$$A_1 = A_2$$

1) In series circuits the *same current* flows through *all parts* of the circuit. I.e. the reading on ammeter A_1 is the same as the reading on ammeter A_2:

$$A_1 = A_2$$

2) The *size* of the current is determined by the *total P.D.* of the cells and the *total resistance* of the circuit: i.e. *I = V/R*.

3) Resistance Adds Up:

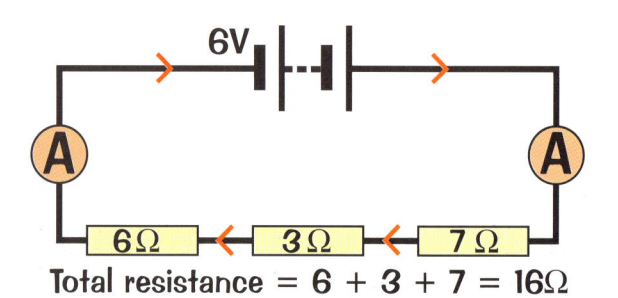

6V

6Ω 3Ω 7Ω

Total resistance = 6 + 3 + 7 = 16Ω

1) In series circuits the *total resistance* is just the *sum* of all the resistances:

$$R = R_1 + R_2 + R_3$$

2) The *bigger* the *resistance* of a component, the bigger its *share* of the *total P.D.*

SEG SYLLABUS — *SECTION ONE — ELECTRICITY AND MAGNETISM*

Series Circuits

Energy in Circuits

Cell Voltages Add Up:

1) There is a bigger potential difference with more cells in series, provided the cells are all *connected* the *same way*.
2) For example when two batteries of voltage 1.5V are *connected in series*, they supply 3V *between them*.

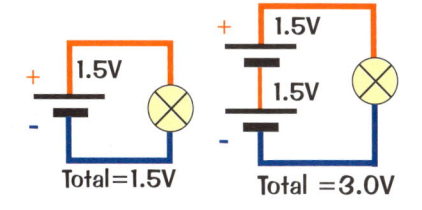

Total=1.5V   Total =3.0V

More Lamps in Series Means Dimmer Lamps:

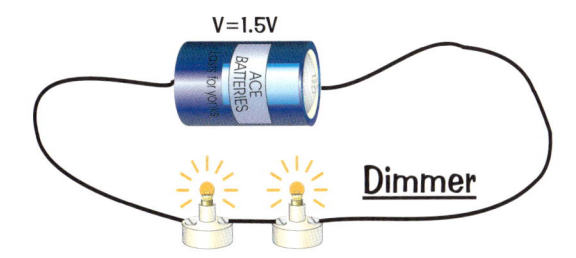

1) If a *lamp* is connected in series with a battery then it lights up with a certain brightness.
2) However with *more lamps* (of the same resistance) connected in series, then all the lamps will light up at a *reduced brightness*.
3) This is because in a *series circuit* the voltage is *shared out* between the components in the circuit.
4) When a *second cell* is connected in series with the first then the brightness of the lamps will *increase* because there is a *bigger source P.D.*

Dimmer

Example on Series Circuits

With the circuit opposite the rules on these two pages apply:
Voltages add to equal the *source voltage*:
$1.5 + 2 + 2.5 = 6V$.
Total resistance is the sum of the resistances in the circuit: $3 + 4 + 5 = 12 \Omega$.
Current flowing through all parts of the circuit $= V/R = 6/12 = 0.5A$.
(If an extra cell was added then the voltage across each resistor would increase).

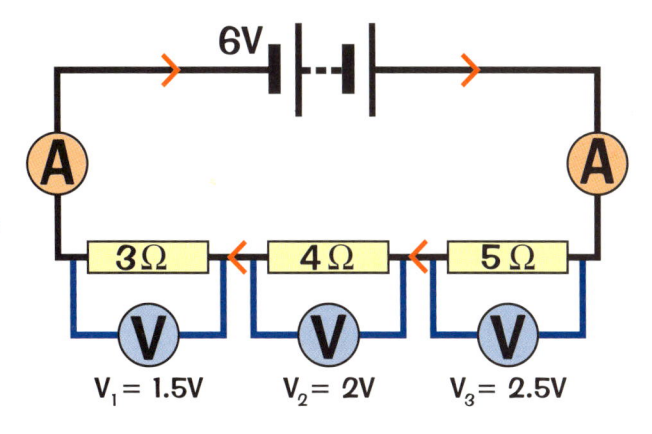

$V_1 = 1.5V$ $V_2 = 2V$ $V_3 = 2.5V$

Christmas Fairy Lights Are Wired in Series

Christmas fairy lights are about the *only* real-life example of things connected in *series*, and we all know what a *pain* they are when the *whole lot go out* just because *one* of the bulbs is slightly dicky. The only *advantage* is that the bulbs can be *very small* because the total 230V is *shared out* between them, so each bulb only has a *small* voltage across it.

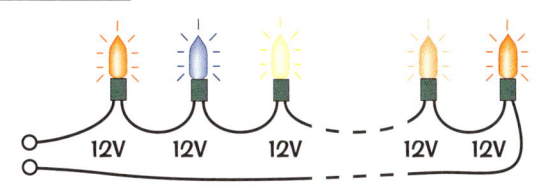

Series circuits — phew, it's just one thing after another...

They really do want you to know the difference between series and parallel circuits. It's not that tricky but you do have to make a real effort to *learn all the details*. That's what these pages are for. Learn all those details, then *cover the pages* and *scribble them all down*. Then try again...

SECTION ONE — ELECTRICITY AND MAGNETISM   SEG SYLLABUS

Parallel Circuits

Energy in Circuits

Parallel circuits are much more *sensible* than series circuits and so they're much more *common* in *real life*.

Parallel Circuits — Independence and Isolation

1) In *parallel circuits*, each component is *separately* connected to the +ve and −ve of the *supply*.
2) If you remove or disconnect *one* of them, it will *hardly affect* the others at all.
3) This is *obviously* how *most* things must be connected, for example in *cars* and in *household electrics*. You have to be able to switch everything on and off *separately*.

P.D. Is the Same Across All Components:

1) In parallel circuits *all* components get the *full source P.D.*, so the voltage is the *same* across all components:

$$V_1 = V_2 = V_3$$

2) This means that *identical bulbs* connected in parallel will all have the *same brightness*.

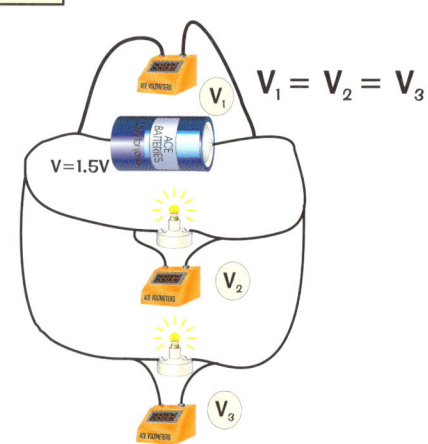

$V_1 = V_2 = V_3$

Current Is Shared Between Branches:

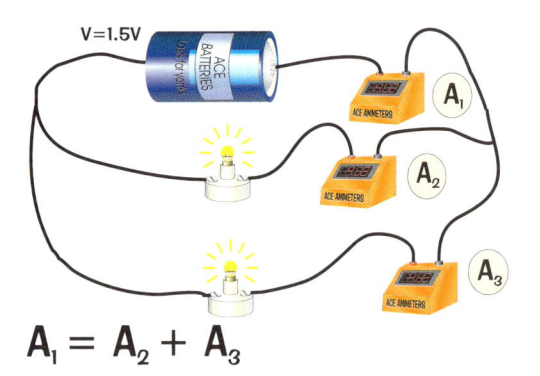

1) In parallel circuits the *total current* flowing around the circuit is equal to the *total* of all the currents in the *separate branches*.

$$A = A_1 + A_2 + A_3$$

2) In a parallel circuit, there are *junctions* where the current either *splits* or *rejoins*. The total current going *into* a junction *always* equals the total current *leaving* — fairly obviously.

$A_1 = A_2 + A_3$

3) If two *identical components* are connected in parallel then the *same current* will flow through each component.

Resistance Is Tricky:

1) The *current* through each component depends on its *resistance*. The *lower* the resistance, the *bigger* the current that'll flow through it.
2) The *total resistance* of the circuit is *tricky to work out*, but it's always *LESS* than that of the branch with the *smallest* resistance.

SEG Syllabus

Section One — Electricity and Magnetism

Parallel Circuits

Energy in Circuits

Parallel Circuits Example

1) The *voltage* across each resistor in the circuit is the same as the *supply voltage*. Each voltmeter will read 6V.

2) The current through each resistor will be *different* because they have different values of *resistance*.

3) The current through the battery is the same as the *sum* of the other currents in the branches.
i.e. $A_1 = A_2 + A_3 + A_4$
$A_1 = 1.5 + 3 + 1 = 5.5A$

4) The *total resistance* in the whole circuit is *less* than that of the *lowest branch*, i.e. lower than 2Ω.

5) The *biggest current* flows through the *middle branch* because that branch has the *lowest resistance*.

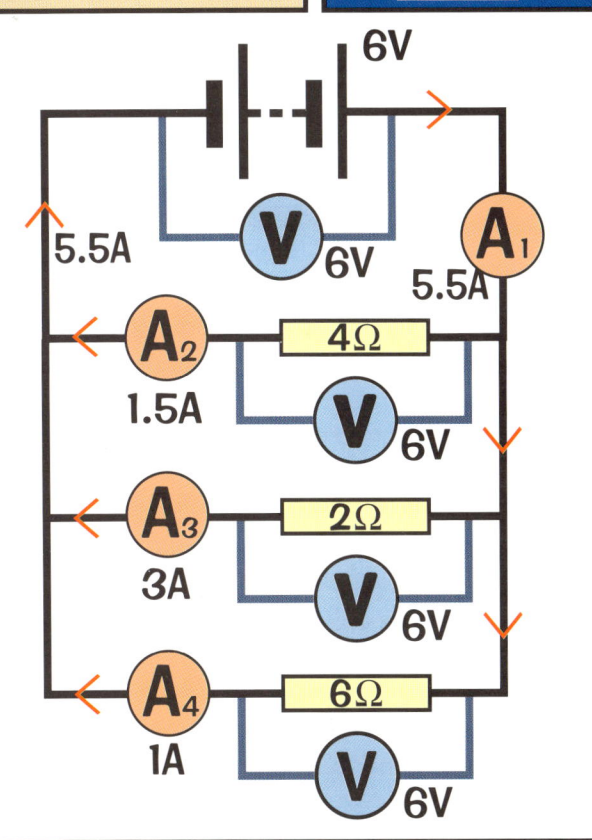

Everything Electrical in a Car Is Connected in Parallel

Parallel connection is *essential* in a car to give these *two features*:

1) Everything can be *turned on and off separately*.
2) Everything always gets the *full voltage* from the battery.

The only *slight effect* is that when you turn *lots of things on*, the lights may go *dim* because the battery can't provide the *full voltage* under *heavy load*. This is normally a *very slight* effect. You can spot the same thing at home when you turn a kettle on, if you watch very carefully.

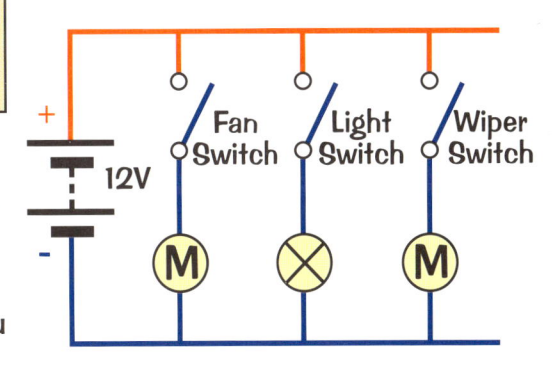

Voltmeters and Ammeters Are Exceptions to the Rule:

1) Ammeters and voltmeters are *exceptions* to the series and parallel rules.
2) Ammeters are *always* connected in *series*, even in a parallel circuit.
3) Voltmeters are *always* connected in *parallel with a component*, even in a series circuit.

Electric circuits — unparalleled dreariness...

Make sure you can scribble down a parallel circuit and know what the advantages are. Learn the five numbered points and the details for connecting ammeters and voltmeters, and also what two features make parallel connection essential in a car. Then *cover the page* and *scribble it*...

SECTION ONE — ELECTRICITY AND MAGNETISM

SEG SYLLABUS

Energy in Circuits

You can look at _electrical circuits_ in _two ways_. The first is in terms of a voltage _pushing the current_ round and the resistances opposing the flow, as on P. 3. The _other way_ of looking at circuits is in terms of _energy transfer_. Learn them _both_ and be ready to tackle questions about _either_.

Energy Is Transferred from Cells and Other Sources

Anything which _supplies electricity_ is also supplying _energy_. So cells, batteries, generators etc. all _transfer energy_ to components in the circuit. _Learn these as examples_:

MOTION: motors   **LIGHT:** light bulbs   **HEAT:** Hairdriers/kettles   **SOUND:** speakers

- Kinetic Energy (M)
- Light Energy
- Cell provides the energy
- Heat Energy
- Sound Energy

All Resistors Produce Heat When Current Flows Through Them

1) This is important. Whenever a _current_ flows through anything with _electrical resistance_ (which is pretty well _everything_) then _electrical energy_ is converted into _heat energy_.
2) The _more current_ that flows, the _more heat_ is produced.

And this Heat can be Useful...

1) A resistor heats the _air_ in a _hairdrier_.
2) A resistor heats the _water_ in an _immersion heater_.
3) The _filament_ of a _light bulb_ is a resistor made from _tungsten_. It gets so hot that it _glows_ — bright enough to light the room.

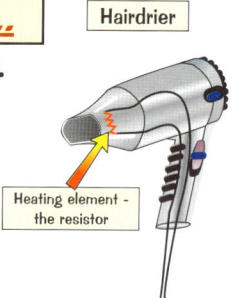

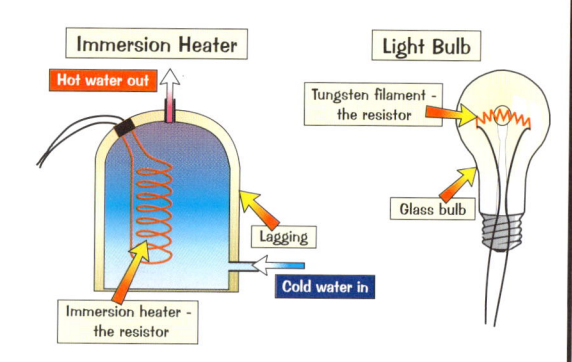

Hairdrier — Heating element - the resistor

Immersion Heater — Hot water out, Lagging, Cold water in, Immersion heater - the resistor

Light Bulb — Tungsten filament - the resistor, Glass bulb

Energy Is Measured in Joules

...and the amount of _heat energy_ given off by _resistance_ is the same as the amount of _electrical energy_ lost by the circuit (assuming of course it doesn't go into other forms like _light_).

Voltage and Energy Change

1) When electrical _charge_ (Q) goes through a _change_ in voltage (V), then _energy_ (E) is _transferred_.
   Energy is _supplied_ to the charge at the _power source_ to raise it through a voltage.
   The charge _gives up_ this energy when it _falls_ through any _voltage drop_ in _components_ elsewhere in the circuit.
   The formula is real simple: $E = QV$

2) The _bigger_ the _change_ in voltage, the _more energy_ is transferred for a _given amount of charge_ passing through the circuit. That means that a battery with a _bigger voltage_ will supply _more energy_ to the circuit for every _coulomb_ of charge that flows round it, because the charge is raised up "_higher_" at the start (see above diagram) — and as the diagram shows, _more energy_ will be _dissipated_ in the circuit too.

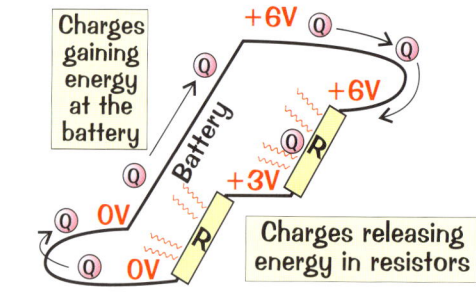

Charges gaining energy at the battery. +6V, +6V, +3V, 0V, 0V. Charges releasing energy in resistors.

$$\frac{E}{Q \times V}$$

Electricity — why does it all turn out so dreary...

I try to make it interesting, really I do. I mean, underneath it all, electricity is pretty good stuff, but somehow every page just seems to end up stuffed full of interminably dreary facts. Well look, _I tried_, OK. It may be dreary but you've just gotta _learn it all_, and that's that.

SEG SYLLABUS — SECTION ONE — ELECTRICITY AND MAGNETISM

Magnetic Fields

Electromagnetic Forces

There's a proper definition of a _magnetic field_ which you really ought to learn:

> A _MAGNETIC FIELD_ is a region where _MAGNETIC MATERIALS_ (like iron and steel) and also _WIRES CARRYING CURRENTS_ experience _A FORCE_ acting on them.

Learn All These Magnetic Field Diagrams, Arrow-Perfect

They're real likely to give you one of these diagrams to do in your Exam.
So make sure you know them, especially which way the _arrows point_ — ALWAYS from N to S!

Bar Magnet

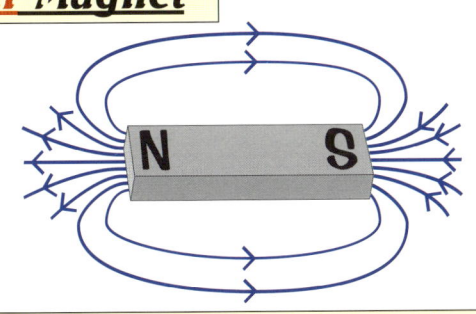

Solenoid

Same field as a bar magnet _outside_.

Strong and uniform field on the _inside_.

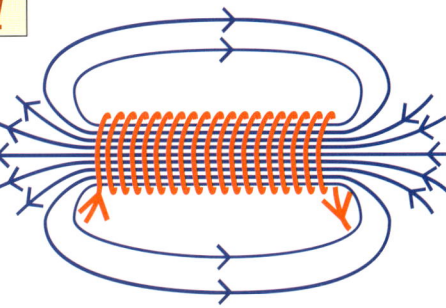

Two Bar Magnets Attracting

Opposite poles ATTRACT, as I'm sure you know.

Two Bar Magnets Repelling

Like poles REPEL, as you must surely know.

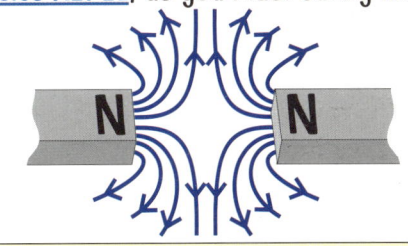

The Earth's Magnetic Field

Note that the _magnetic poles_ are _opposite_ to the _Geographic Poles_, i.e. the _south pole_ is at the _North Pole_ — if you see what I mean! That way the _north pole_ of a _compass needle_ points to it.

The Magnetic Field Round a Current-Carrying Wire

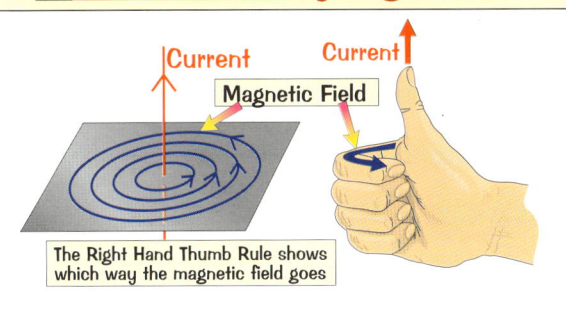

The Right Hand Thumb Rule shows which way the magnetic field goes

The Poles of a Solenoid

If you imagine looking directly into one end of a solenoid, the _direction of current flow_ tells you whether it's the _N or S pole_ you're looking at, as shown by the _two diagrams_ opposite. Make sure you remember those diagrams.

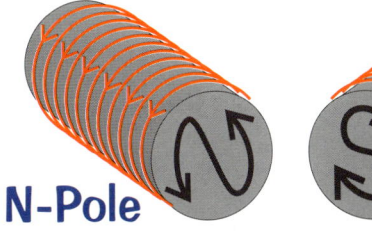

N-Pole   S-Pole

Magnetic fields — there's no getting away from them...

Mmm, this is a nice easy page for you isn't it. Learn the definition of what a magnetic field is and the six field diagrams. But pay loads of attention to what way the arrows are pointing — so many people lose marks on that. Once you think you know it, just _cover the page_ and _scribble_.

SECTION ONE — ELECTRICITY AND MAGNETISM   SEG SYLLABUS

Electromagnets

Electromagnetic Forces

An Electromagnet Is Just a Coil of Wire with an Iron Core

1) *Electromagnets* are simply a *solenoid* (just a *coil of wire*) with a piece of *"soft"* iron inside.
2) When *current flows* through the *wires* of the solenoid it creates a *magnetic field* around it.
3) The *soft iron core* has the effect of *increasing* the *magnetic field strength*.
4) *"Soft"* just means that it *doesn't retain its magnetism*, so that when the current is turned off, the *magnetism disappears* with it. That means that you can turn the electromagnet *off*.

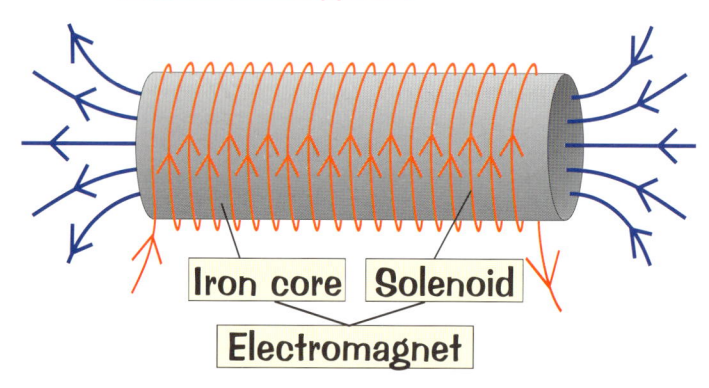

Iron core **Solenoid**
Electromagnet

1) The *magnetic field* around an *electromagnet* is just like the one round a *bar magnet*, only *stronger*.
2) This means that the *ends* of a *solenoid* act like the *north pole* and *south pole* of a bar magnet.
3) Pretty obviously, if the direction of the *current* is *reversed*, the N and S poles will *swap ends*.

The STRENGTH of an ELECTROMAGNET depends on THREE FACTORS:
1) The size of the **CURRENT**.
2) The number of **TURNS** the coil has.
3) What the **CORE** is made of.

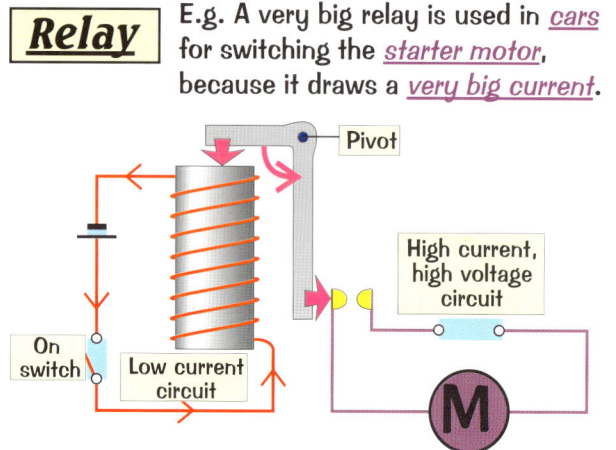

Relay
E.g. A very big relay is used in *cars* for switching the *starter motor*, because it draws a *very big current*.

1) A *relay* is a device which uses a *low current* circuit to *switch* a *high current* circuit on/off.
2) When the switch in the low current circuit is *closed* it turns the electromagnet *ON* which *attracts* the *iron rocker*.
3) The rocker *pivots* and *closes* the contacts in the high current circuit.
4) When the low current switch is *opened*, the electromagnet *stops* pulling, the rocker returns, and the high current circuit is *broken* again.

Electric Bell
These are used in schools to stress everyone out.

1) When the switch is *closed*, the electromagnets are turned *on*.
2) They pull the iron arm *DOWN* which *clangs* the bell, but at the same time *breaks* the contact, which immediately *turns off* the electromagnets.
3) The arm then *springs back*, which *closes* the *contact*, and off we go again...
4) The whole sequence happens *very* quickly, maybe *10 times a second*, so the bell sounds like a continuous *"brrriiiinnngg"* sound. Nice.

Electromagnets really irritate me — I just get solenoid with them...

This is all very basic information, and really quite memorable I'd have thought. Learn the headings and diagrams first, then *cover the page* and *scribble them down*. Then gradually fill in the other details. *Keep looking back and checking*. Try to learn *all* the points. Lovely innit.

SEG SYLLABUS — SECTION ONE — ELECTRICITY AND MAGNETISM

The Electric Motor

Electromagnetic Forces

Anything carrying a *current* in a *magnetic field* will experience a *force*. There are *three important cases*:

A Current in a Magnetic Field Experiences a Force

The two tests below demonstrate the *force* on a *current-carrying wire* placed in a *magnetic field*. The *force* gets *bigger* if either the *current* or the *magnetic field* is made bigger.

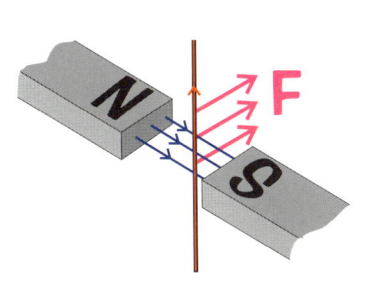

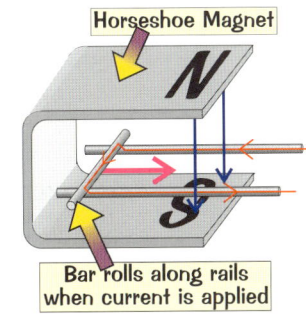

1) Note that in *both cases* the *force* on the wire is at *90°* to both the *wire* and to the *magnetic field*.
2) You can always *predict* which way the *force* will act using *Fleming's LHR* as shown below.
3) To experience the *full force*, the *wire* has to be at *90°* to the *magnetic field*.
4) The *direction* of the force is *reversed* if either:
   a) the direction of the *current* is reversed.
   b) the direction of the *magnetic field* is reversed.

The Simple Electric Motor

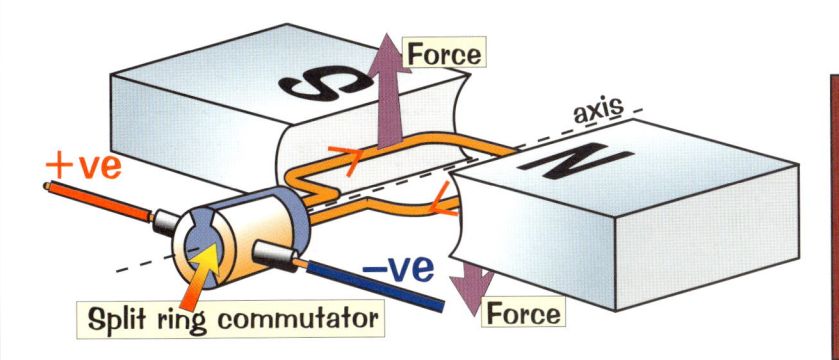

4 Factors That Speed It Up
1) More **CURRENT**
2) More **TURNS** on the coil
3) **STRONGER MAGNETIC FIELD**
4) A **SOFT IRON CORE** in the coil

1) The diagram shows the *forces* acting on the two *side arms* of the *coil*.
2) These forces are just the *usual forces* which act on *any current* in a *magnetic field*.
3) Because the coil is on a *spindle* and the forces act *one up* and *one down*, it *rotates*.
4) The direction of the motor can be *reversed* either by swapping the *polarity* of the *DC supply*, or by swapping the *magnetic poles* over.

Fleming's Left Hand Rule Tells You Which Way the Force Acts

1) They could test if you can do this, so *practise it*.
2) Using your *left hand*, point your *First finger* in the direction of the *Field* and your *seCond finger* in the direction of the *Current*.
3) Your *thuMb* will then point in the direction of the *force* (*Motion*).

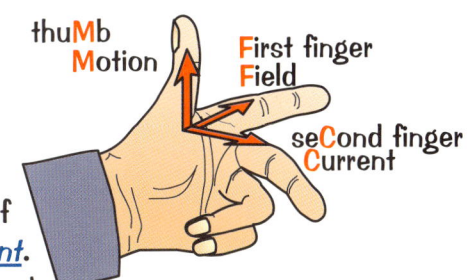

thuMb — Motion
First finger — Field
seCond finger — Current

Fleming — how many broken wrists has he caused already...

Same old routine here. *Learn all the details*, diagrams and all, then *cover the page* and *scribble it all down* again *from memory*. I presume you do realise that you should be scribbling it down as scruffy as you like — because all you're trying to do is make sure that you really do *know it*.

SECTION ONE — ELECTRICITY AND MAGNETISM   SEG SYLLABUS

Electromagnetic Induction

Sounds terrifying, but it really isn't that complicated. For some reason though they use the word "induction" rather than "creation", but it amounts to the same thing. I reckon they're just trying to confuse you.

ELECTROMAGNETIC INDUCTION: The creation of a **VOLTAGE** (and/or current) in a wire that is in a **CHANGING MAGNETIC FIELD**.

1) Of course if the field didn't change, but the wire moved through it, then from the wire's point of view it would still look like the field was changing.
2) So this also generates a voltage in the wire.

This means there's *two* different situations in which you get EM induction. You need to know about *both* of them:

a) The conductor moves across a magnetic field and "cuts" through the field lines (as in the diagram to the right — a coil is moved between the poles of a magnet).

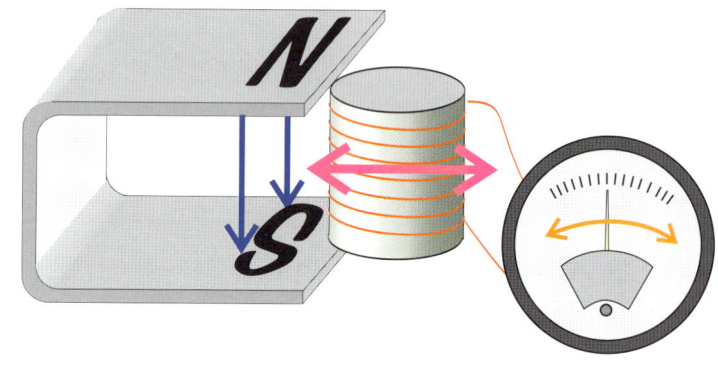

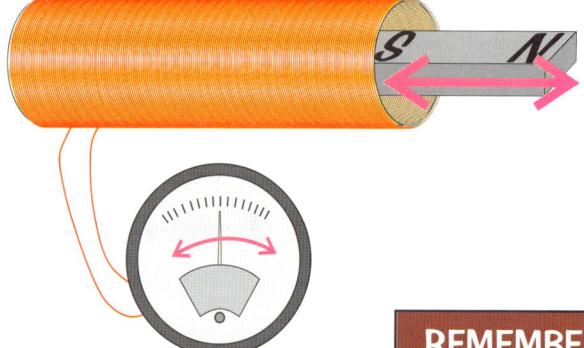

b) The magnetic field through a closed coil **CHANGES**, i.e. gets bigger or smaller or reverses (as in the diagram to the left — a magnet is moved into or out of a stationary coil).

REMEMBER THESE POINTS:

1) If the direction of movement is reversed, then the voltage/current will be reversed too.
2) The current will also be reversed if the opposite pole of the magnet is shoved into the coil.

The Dynamo Principle

A voltage and/or current will be produced in a coil when there is relative movement between it and a magnetic field.

This is a pretty handy effect, as it's used in generators to produce our mains electricity. It's called the DYNAMO PRINCIPLE.

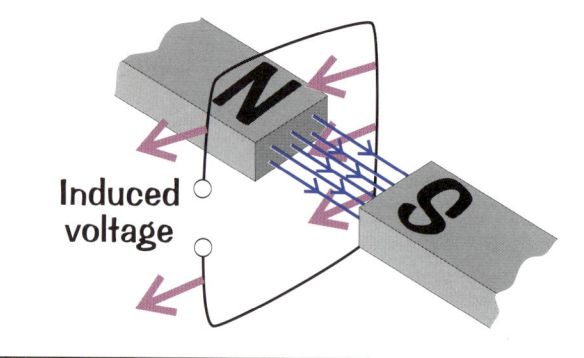

Four Factors Affect the Size of the Induced Voltage:

1) The **STRENGTH** of the **MAGNET**
2) The **SPEED** of movement
3) The **number of TURNS** on the **COIL**
4) The **AREA** of the **COIL**

Electromagnetic induction — pretty tricky stuff...

Electromagnetic induction gets my vote for "Definitely Most Tricky Topic in GCSE Double Science". If it wasn't so important maybe you wouldn't have to bother learning it. The trouble is this is how all our electricity is generated. So it's pretty important. *Learn and scribble*...

SEG SYLLABUS — SECTION ONE — ELECTRICITY AND MAGNETISM

Electromagnetic Induction

Generators

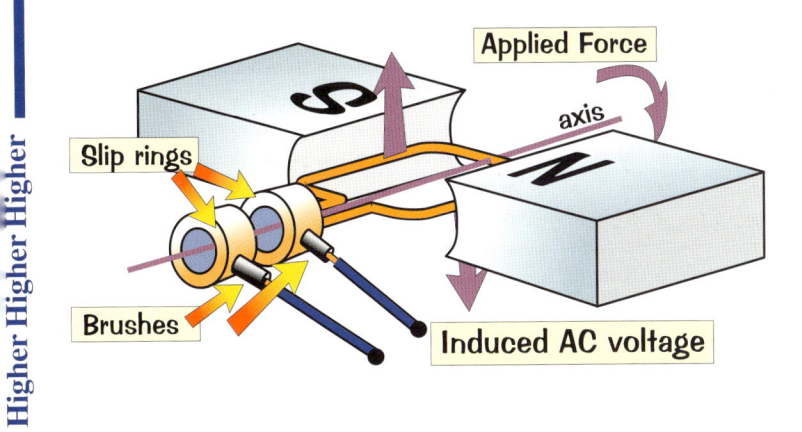

1) Generators *rotate* a coil in a *magnetic field* to generate electricity by the *dynamo principle* (see P. 14).
2) Their *construction* is pretty much like a *motor*.
3) The *difference* is the *slip rings*, which are in *constant contact* with the brushes so the contacts *don't swap* every ½ turn.
4) This means they produce *AC voltage*.
5) Note that *faster* revs produce not only *more* peaks, but *higher* overall voltage too.

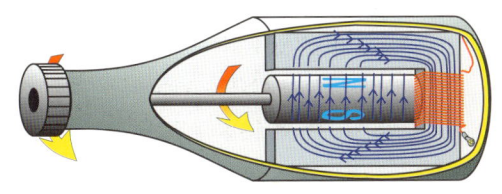

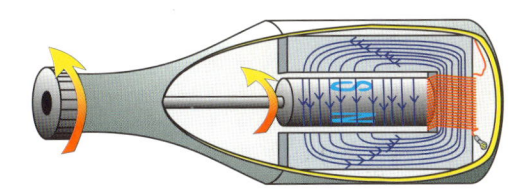

Dynamos

Dynamos are slightly different from *generators* because they rotate the *magnet* instead of the coil. The *coil* now *surrounds* the magnet and *doesn't move*. This still causes the *field through the coil* to *swap* every half turn, so the output is *just the same* — an *alternating current* (*AC*).

The Two Types of Current

Direct Current (DC)

1) The *current* from a *battery* stays *constant* if the circuit doesn't change.
2) It flows in just *one direction* — from the *positive to the negative* terminal.
3) Since it has only one direction, it is called *direct current* (*DC*).

Direct Current at 2V in one direction

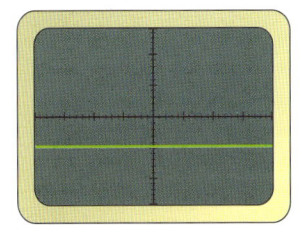

Direct Current at 1V in the other direction

Alternating Current (AC)

1) *Mains electricity* on the other hand is *alternating current* (*AC*).
2) This means that the *direction* of the current *changes continually*.
3) The *frequency* of the supply tells you *how many times it changes* from one direction to the other and *back again* each *second*.

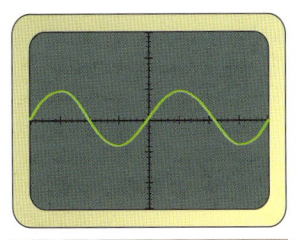

Alternating Current at 1V at one frequency

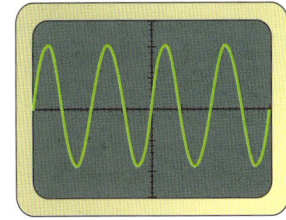

Alternating Current at 2V at twice the frequency

This page could generate a bit of a headache...

Well, at least there's only *two* types of current for you to learn about. You'd better make sure you know the cathode ray oscilloscope stuff though — they like to throw that sort of thing into Exams. And of course you know the best way to *learn* it — *cover and scribble*...

SECTION ONE — ELECTRICITY AND MAGNETISM

Transformers

Transformers use Electromagnetic Induction. So they will only work on AC.

Transformers Change the Voltage — but Only AC Voltages

They are used in the production and distribution of our mains electricity, and there's two types:
1) Step-up transformers step the voltage up. They have more turns on the secondary coil.
2) Step-down transformers step the voltage down. They have fewer turns on the secondary. They drop the voltage from 400,000V to a "safe" 230V for our homes.

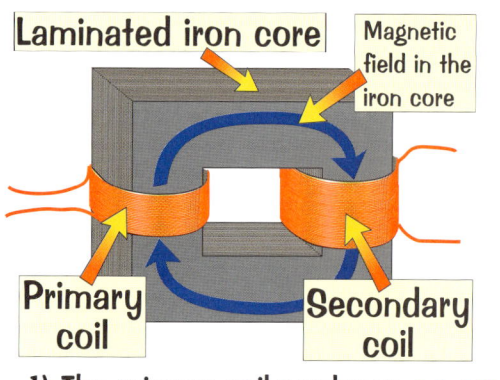

1) The laminated iron core is purely for transferring the magnetic field from the primary coil to the secondary.
2) The iron core is laminated with layers of insulation to reduce the eddy currents which heat it up, and therefore waste energy.

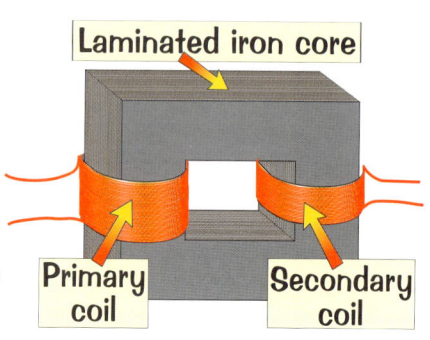

1) The primary coil produces a magnetic field which stays within the iron core and this means it all passes through the secondary coil.
2) Because there is alternating current (AC) in the primary coil, this means that the magnetic field in the iron core is reversing (50 times a second, usually) — i.e. it's a changing field.
3) This rapidly changing magnetic field is then experienced by the secondary coil and this induces an alternating voltage in it — electromagnetic induction of a voltage in fact.
4) The relative number of turns on the two coils determines whether the voltage created in the secondary is greater or less than the voltage in the primary.
5) If you supplied DC to the primary, you'd get NOTHING out of the secondary at all. Sure, there'd still be a field in the iron core, but it wouldn't be constantly changing, so there'd be no induction in the secondary because you need a changing field to induce a voltage. Don't you! So don't forget it — transformers only work with AC. They won't work with DC at all.

The Transformer Equation — Use It Either Way Up

In words: The RATIO OF TURNS on the two coils equals the RATIO OF THEIR VOLTAGES.

$$\frac{\text{Primary Voltage}}{\text{Secondary Voltage}} = \frac{\text{Number of turns on Primary}}{\text{Number of turns on Secondary}}$$

$$\frac{V_P}{V_S} = \frac{N_P}{N_S}$$

or

$$\frac{V_S}{V_P} = \frac{N_S}{N_P}$$

Well, it's just another formula. You stick in the numbers you've got and work out the one that's left. It's real useful to remember you can write it either way up — this example's much trickier algebra-wise if you start with V_S on the bottom...

EXAMPLE: A transformer has 40 turns on the primary and 800 on the secondary. If the input voltage is 1,000V find the output voltage.

ANSWER: $V_S/V_P = N_S/N_P$ so $V_S/1{,}000 = 800/40$ $V_S = 1{,}000 \times (800/40) = \underline{20{,}000V}$

The ubiquitous iron core — where would we be without it...

Besides their iron core, transformers have lots of other important details which also need to be learnt. You'll need practise with that tricky equation too. It's unusual because it can't be put into formula triangles, but other than that the method is the same. Just practise.

SEG SYLLABUS   SECTION ONE — ELECTRICITY AND MAGNETISM

The National Grid

Transformers

1) The _National Grid_ is the _network_ of pylons and cables which _covers_ the whole of Britain.
2) It takes electricity from the _power stations_, to just where it's needed in _homes_ and _industry_.
3) It enables power to be _generated_ anywhere on the grid, and to then be _supplied_ anywhere else on the grid.

All Power Stations Are Pretty Much the Same

They all have a _boiler_ of some sort that makes _steam_, which drives a _turbine_, which drives a _generator_. The generator produces _electricity_ (by _induction_) by _rotating_ an _electromagnet_ within coils of wire (see P. 15).

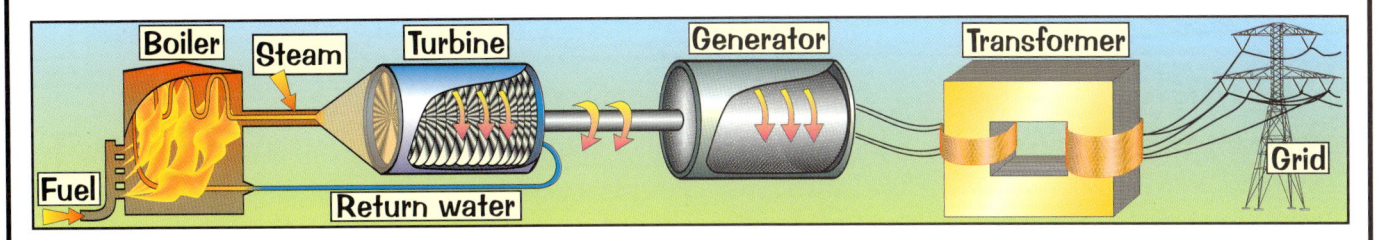

Learn all these features of the NATIONAL GRID — power stations, transformers, pylons, etc.:

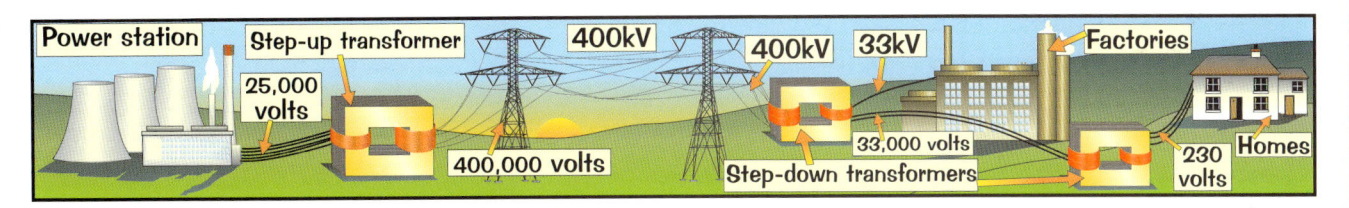

Pylon Cables Are at 400,000 V to Keep the Current Low

You need to understand why the VOLTAGE is so HIGH and why it's AC. Learn these points:

1) The formula for _power supplied_ is: _Power = Voltage × Current_ or: $P = V \times I$
2) So to transmit a _lot_ of power, you either need high _voltage_ or high _current_.
3) The problem with _high current_ is the _loss_ (as heat) due to the _resistance_ of the cables.
4) The formula for _heat loss_ due to resistance in the cables is: $P = I^2R$.
5) Because of the I^2 bit, if the current is _10 times_ bigger, the losses will be _100 times_ bigger.
6) So it's much _cheaper_ to boost the voltage up to _400,000V_ and keep the current _very low_.
7) This requires _transformers_ as well as _big_ pylons with _huge_ insulators, but it's still _cheaper_.
8) The transformers have to _step_ the voltage _up_ at one end, for _efficient_ transmission, and then bring it back down to _safe_ useable levels at the other end.
9) This is why it has to be _AC_ on the National Grid — so that the _transformers_ will work!

You can also reduce the heat loss by increasing the thickness of the cable (which reduces the resistance). But thicker cable costs more, so a compromise has to be made.

400,000 volts? — that could give you a bit of a buzz...

Quite a few tricky details on this page. The power station and National Grid are easy enough, but fully explaining why pylon cables are at 400,000V is a bit trickier — but you do need to learn it. When you watch TV think of the route the electricity has to travel. _Scribble it down_.

SECTION ONE — ELECTRICITY AND MAGNETISM   SEG SYLLABUS

Electricity in the Home

Mains Electricity

Now then, did you know... electricity is dangerous. It can kill you. Well just watch out for it, that's all.

Plugs and Cables — Learn the Safety Features

Get the Wiring Right:

1) The right coloured wire to each pin, and firmly screwed in.
2) No bare wires showing inside the plug.
3) Cable grip tightly fastened over the cable outer layer.

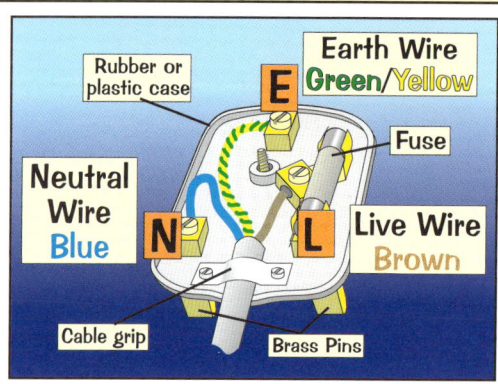

Plug diagram: Rubber or plastic case, Earth Wire Green/Yellow (E), Fuse, Neutral Wire Blue (N), Live Wire Brown (L), Cable grip, Brass Pins

Plug Features:

1) The metal parts are made of copper or brass because these are very good conductors.
2) The case, cable grip and cable insulation are all made of plastic because this is a really good insulator and is flexible too.
3) This all keeps the electricity flowing where it should.

Earthing and Fuses Prevent Fires and Shocks

The LIVE WIRE alternates between a HIGH +VE AND −VE VOLTAGE, with an average of about 230V. The NEUTRAL WIRE is always at 0V. Electricity normally flows in and out through the live and neutral wires only. The EARTH WIRE and fuse (or circuit breaker) are just for safety and work together like this:

1) If a fault develops in which the live somehow touches the metal case, then because the case is earthed, a big current flows in through the live, through the case and out down the earth wire.
2) This surge in current blows the fuse, which cuts off the live supply.
3) This isolates the whole appliance, making it impossible to get an electric shock from the case. It also prevents the risk of fire caused by the heating effect of a large current.
4) Fuses should be rated as near as possible to, but just higher than, the normal operating current (See P. 19).

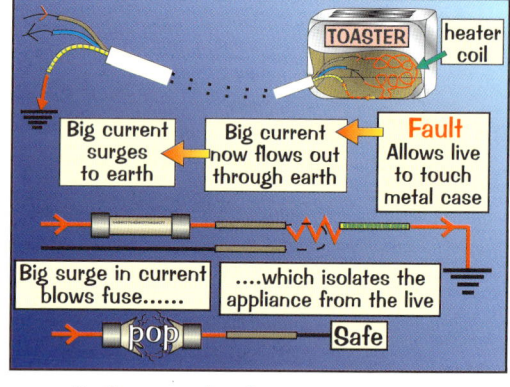

Diagram: TOASTER with heater coil — Fault Allows live to touch metal case; Big current now flows out through earth; Big current surges to earth; Big surge in current blows fuse...... pop ....which isolates the appliance from the live; Safe

All appliances with metal cases must be "earthed" to avoid the danger of electric shock. "Earthing" just means the metal case must be attached to the earth wire in the cable.
If the appliance has a plastic casing and no metal parts showing then it's said to be DOUBLE INSULATED. Anything with double insulation like that doesn't need an earth wire, just a live and neutral.

Circuit Breakers Act as Resettable Fuses

1) The current flowing in the live and neutral wires should normally be the same.
2) But if a fault develops, some current might flow to earth — possibly through someone.
3) Then there'll be less current flowing in the neutral wire than in the live wire.
4) A RESIDUAL CIRCUIT BREAKER compares the currents in these two wires, and shuts off the supply (breaks the circuit) if there's a difference.

Circuit breakers have two main advantages over fuses:
1) If the circuit is broken, you don't have to replace a fuse — merely reset the circuit breaker.
2) They switch the current off much faster than a fuse, so they're safer. They're commonly used with high risk appliances like lawnmowers for this reason.

Some people are so careless with electricity — it's shocking...

A few too many words on this page I think. Just so much to learn. Make sure you know all the details for wiring a plug. Trickiest of all, make sure you understand how earthing and fuses act together to make things safe. Learnt it all? Good-O. Cover the page and scribble it down.

SEG Syllabus — SECTION ONE — ELECTRICITY AND MAGNETISM

Electricity in the Home

Power/Mains Electricity

Electrical Power and Fuse Ratings

1) <u>Electrical Power</u> is defined as the <u>rate of transfer of electrical energy</u>. It is measured in <u>watts</u> (W), which is just <u>joules per second</u> (J/s).
2) The standard formula for <u>electrical power</u> is: P=VI
3) If you <u>combine</u> it with <u>V=I×R</u>, and replace the "V" with "I×R", you get: P=I²R
4) If instead you use V=I×R and replace the "I" with "V/R", you get: P=V²/R
5) You <u>choose</u> which <u>one</u> of these formulae to use, purely and simply by seeing which one contains the <u>three quantities</u> that are <u>involved</u> in the problem you're looking at.

Calculating Fuse Ratings — Always Use the Formula: "P=VI"

Most electrical goods indicate their <u>power rating</u> and <u>voltage rating</u>. To work out the <u>FUSE</u> needed, you need to work out the <u>current</u> that the item will normally use. That means using "P=VI", or rather, "I=P/V".

EXAMPLE: A hairdrier is rated at 240V, 1.1kW. Find the fuse needed.
ANSWER: I = P/V = 1100/240 = 4.6A. Normally, the fuse should be rated just a little higher than the normal current, so a 5 amp fuse is ideal for this one.

Reading Your Electricity Meter and Working Out the Bill

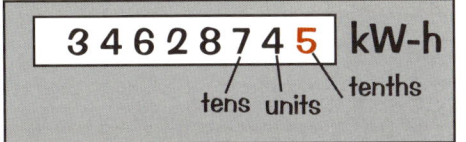

3 4 6 2 8 7 4 5 kW-h
tens units tenths

The reading on your meter shows the <u>total number of units</u> (kW-h) used since the meter was fitted. Each bill is worked out from the <u>INCREASE</u> in the meter reading since it was <u>last read</u> for the previous bill.

Kilowatt-Hours (kW-h) Are "UNITS" of Energy

1) Your electricity meter counts the number of "<u>UNITS</u>" used.
2) A "<u>UNIT</u>" is otherwise known as a <u>kilowatt-hour</u>, or <u>kW-h</u>.
3) A "<u>kW-h</u>" might sound like a unit of power, but it's not — it's an <u>amount of energy</u>.

> A <u>KILOWATT-HOUR</u> is the amount of electrical energy used by a <u>1 KW APPLIANCE</u> left on for <u>1 HOUR</u>.

4) Make sure you can turn <u>1 kW-h</u> into <u>3,600,000 joules</u> like this:
     "E=P×t" = 1kW × 1 hour = 1,000W × 3,600 secs = <u>3,600,000 J</u> (=3.6 MJ)
(The formula is "Energy = Power×time", and the units must be converted to <u>watts</u> and <u>seconds</u> first).

The Two Easy Formulae for Calculating the Cost of Electricity

These must surely be the two most <u>trivial and obvious</u> formulae you'll ever see:

No. of <u>UNITS</u> (kW-h) used = <u>POWER</u> (in kW) × <u>TIME</u> (in hours)	Units = kW × hours
<u>COST</u> = No. of <u>UNITS</u> × <u>PRICE</u> per UNIT	Cost = Units × Price

EXAMPLE: Find the cost of leaving a 60W light bulb on for a) 30 minutes   b) one year.
ANSWER: a) <u>No. of UNITS = kW × hours</u> = 0.06kW × ½hr = 0.03 units.
            <u>Cost = UNITS × price per UNIT</u> (6.3p) = 0.03 × 6.3p = <u>0.189p</u> for 30 mins.
       b) <u>No. of UNITS = kW × hours</u> = 0.06kW × (24×365)hr = 525.6 units.
            <u>Cost = UNITS × price per UNIT</u> (6.3p) = 525.6 × 6.3p = <u>£33.11</u> for one year.

N.B. Always turn the <u>power</u> into <u>kW</u> (not watts) and the <u>time</u> into <u>hours</u> (not minutes).

Kilowa Towers — the best lit hotel in Hawaii...

This page has five sections and you need to learn the stuff in all of them. Start by memorising the headings, then learn the details under each heading. Then <u>cover the page</u> and <u>scribble down</u> what you know. Check back and see what you missed, and then <u>try again</u>. And keep trying.

SECTION ONE — ELECTRICITY AND MAGNETISM   SEG SYLLABUS

Revision Summary for Section One

Electricity and magnetism. What fun. This is definitely Physics at its most grisly. The big problem with Physics in general is that usually there's nothing to "see". You're told that there's a current flowing or a magnetic field lurking, but there's nothing you can actually see with your eyes. That's what makes it so difficult. To get to grips with Physics you have to get used to learning about things that you can't see. Try these questions and see how well you're doing.

1) What is static electricity? What is nearly always the cause of it building up?
2) Which particles move when static builds up, and which ones don't?
3) Give *one* example of static being: a) helpful b) a little joker c) terrorist.
4) What's the unit used for electric charge. What's the formula used to calculate it?
5) Describe what current, voltage and resistance are. What carries current in metals?
6) Sketch the four standard V-I graphs and explain their shapes. How do you get R from them?
7) Scribble down the 10 circuit symbols that you know, with their names of course.
8) Write down two facts about: a) diode b) LDR c) thermistor.
9) Sketch out the standard circuit for testing components, with all the details. Describe how it's used.
10) Sketch a typical series circuit and say why it is a series circuit, not a parallel one.
11) State five rules about the current, voltage and resistance in a series circuit.
12) Give examples of lights wired in series and wired in parallel and explain the main differences.
13) Sketch a typical parallel circuit, showing voltmeter and ammeter positions.
14) State five rules about the current, voltage and resistance in a parallel circuit.
15) Draw a circuit diagram of part of a car's electrics, and explain why they are in parallel.
16) What are the four types of energy that electricity can easily be converted into?
17) Sketch a view of a circuit to explain the formula "E=QV". Which dull definitions go with it?
18) Sketch magnetic fields for: a) a bar magnet, b) a solenoid, c) two magnets attracting,
    d) two magnets repelling, e) the Earth's magnetic field, f) a current-carrying wire.
19) What is an electromagnet made from? Explain how to work out the polarity of the ends.
20) What is meant by magnetically "soft"?
21) Sketch and give details of: a) relay b) electric bell.
22) Sketch two demos of the motor effect. Sketch a simple motor and list four ways to speed it up.
23) Describe the three details of Fleming's left hand rule. What is it used for?
24) Give the definition of electromagnetic induction. Sketch three cases in which it occurs.
25) List the four factors that affect the size of the induced voltage. State the Dynamo principle.
26) Sketch a generator with all the details. Describe how it works, and how a dynamo works.
27) State the two different types of current. List the basic properties of each.
28) Draw what happens to an oscilloscope trace when the voltage is doubled for each type of current.
29) Sketch the two types of transformer, and highlight the main details. Explain how they work.
30) Write down the transformer equation. Do your own worked example — it's ace practice.
31) Sketch a typical power station and the National Grid, and explain why it's at 400kV.
32) Sketch a properly wired plug. Explain how fuses work.
33) Explain fully how earthing works. How does a residual circuit breaker work?
34) Define electrical power, and state its formula.
35) Explain how you would decide what fuse to use for a given electrical appliance.
36) Sketch an electricity meter and explain exactly what the number on it represents.
37) What's a kilowatt-hour? What are the two easy formulae for finding the cost of electricity?
38) Find:
    a) The current when a resistance of 96Ω is connected to a battery of 12V.
    b) The charge passed when a current of 2A flows for 2 minutes.
    c) The power output of a heater that provides 77kJ of heat energy in 4 mins.
    d) The resistance of a hairdrier that draws 10A and gives out 1.4kW.
    e) The energy transferred in 2 minutes by a kettle of power rating 2kW.

FORCES AND MOTION

Speed and Velocity

Speed and Velocity Are Both Just: HOW FAST YOU'RE GOING

Speed and velocity are both measured in m/s (or km/h or mph). They both simply say how fast you're going, but there's a subtle difference between them that you need to know:

SPEED is just **HOW FAST** you're going (e.g. 30mph or 20m/s) with no regard to the direction.
VELOCITY however must **ALSO** have the **DIRECTION** specified, e.g. 30mph *north* or 20m/s, 060°

Seems kinda fussy I know, but they expect you to remember that distinction, so there you go.

Speed, Distance and Time — the Formula:

$$\text{Speed} = \frac{\text{Distance}}{\text{Time}}$$

You really ought to get pretty slick with this very easy formula.
As usual the formula triangle version makes it all a bit of a breeze.
You just need to try and think up some interesting word for remembering the order of the letters in the triangle, s^d t. Errm... sedit, perhaps... well, you think up your own.

EXAMPLE: A cat skulks 20m in 35s. Find a) its speed b) how long it takes to skulk 75m.
ANSWER: Using the formula triangle: a) s = d/t = 20/35 = **0.57m/s**
b) t = d/s = 75/0.57 = 131s = **2 min 11 sec**

A lot of the time we tend to use the words "speed" and "velocity" interchangeably.
For example to calculate velocity you'd just use the above formula for speed.

Distance-Time Graphs

Very Important Notes:

1) **GRADIENT = SPEED**.
2) *Flat* sections are where it's *stopped*.
3) The *steeper* the graph, the *faster* it's going.
4) *Downhill* sections mean it's *coming back* toward its starting point.
5) *Curves* represent *acceleration* or deceleration.
6) A *steepening* curve means it's *speeding up* (increasing gradient).
7) A *levelling off* curve means it's *slowing down* (decreasing gradient).

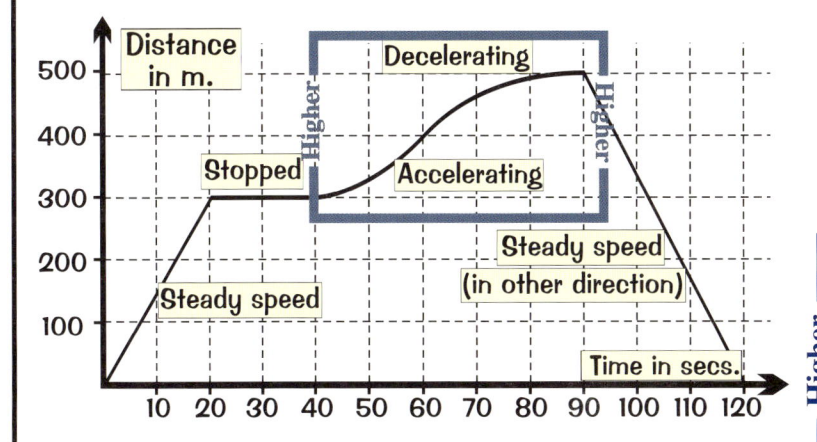

Calculating Speed from a Distance-Time Graph — It's Just the Gradient

For example the speed of the *return* section of the graph is:
Speed = gradient = vertical/horizontal = 500/30 = **16.7 m/s**

Don't forget that you have to use the scales of the axes to work out the gradient. *Don't* measure in *cm*!

Understanding speed — it can be an uphill struggle...

Make sure you know the difference between speed and velocity — it's a favourite way to catch you out in Exams. And as for those distance-time graphs, they can be real tricky — unless you make a real effort to *learn all the numbered points*. So what are you waiting for... *Enjoy*.

SECTION TWO — FORCES AND MOTION

Forces and Acceleration

Force and Acceleration

A _force_ is simply a _push_ or a _pull_. There are only _six_ different forces for you to know about:

1) GRAVITY or WEIGHT always acting straight _downwards_.
2) REACTION FORCE from a _surface_, usually acting _straight upwards_.
3) THRUST or PUSH or PULL due to an engine or rocket _speeding something up_.
4) DRAG or AIR RESISTANCE or FRICTION which is _slowing the thing down_.
5) LIFT due to an _aeroplane wing_.
6) TENSION in a _rope_ or _cable_.

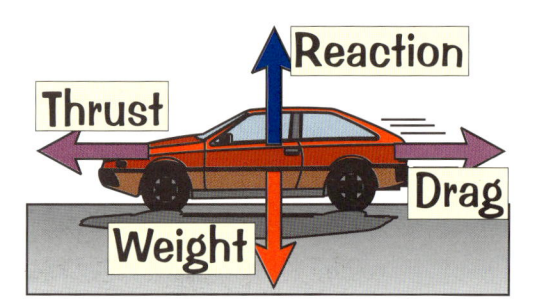

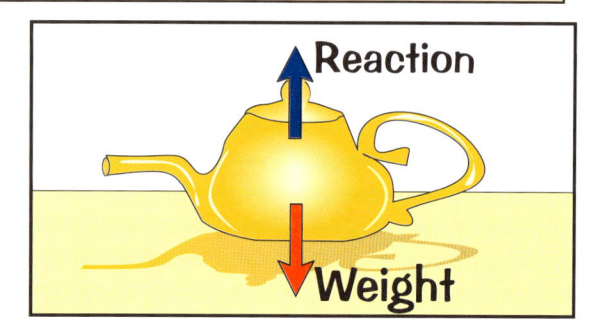

All Forces Are Measured in Newtons

That's _newtons_ with symbol _N_. i.e. the _force_ of gravity on an object of _1kg_ will be _10N_.

Acceleration Is How Quickly You're Speeding Up

Acceleration is definitely _NOT_ the same as _velocity_ or _speed_.
Every time you read or write the word _acceleration_, remind yourself: "_acceleration_ is COMPLETELY DIFFERENT from _velocity_. Acceleration is how _quickly_ the velocity is _changing_."
Velocity is a simple idea. Acceleration is altogether more _subtle_, which is why it's _confusing_.

Acceleration — the Formula:

$$\text{Acceleration} = \frac{\text{Change in Velocity}}{\text{Time Taken}}$$

$\frac{\Delta V}{a \times t}$

Well, it's _just another formula_. Just like all the others. Three things in a _formula triangle_. Mind you, there are _two_ tricky things with this one. First there's the "ΔV", which means working out the "_change in velocity_", as shown in the example below, rather than just putting a _simple value_ for speed or velocity in. Secondly there's the _units_ of acceleration which are m/s². _Not m/s_, which is _velocity_, but m/s². Got it? No? Let's try once more: _Not m/s_, but _m/s²_.

EXAMPLE: A skulking cat accelerates from 2m/s to 6m/s in 5.6s. Find its acceleration.
ANSWER: Using the formula triangle: $a = \Delta V/t = (6 - 2) / 5.6 = 4 \div 5.6 =$ _0.71 m/s²_
All pretty basic stuff I'd say.

Velocity and acceleration — learn the difference...

It's true — some people don't realise that velocity and acceleration are totally different things. Hard to believe I know — all part of the great mystery and tragedy of life I suppose. Anyway. Learn the definitions and the formulae, _cover the page_ and _scribble it all down again_.

SEG SYLLABUS   SECTION TWO — FORCES AND MOTION

Laws of Motion

Force and Acceleration

Around about the time of the Great Plague in the 1660s, a chap called <u>Isaac Newton</u> worked out the <u>Three Laws of Motion</u>. At first they might seem kind of obscure or irrelevant, but to be perfectly blunt, if you can't understand these <u>three simple laws</u> then you'll never fully understand <u>forces and motion</u>:

First Law — Balanced Forces Mean No Change in Velocity

So long as the forces on an object are all <u>**BALANCED**</u>, then it'll just <u>**STAY STILL**</u>, or else if it's already moving it'll just carry on at the <u>**SAME VELOCITY**</u> — so long as the forces are all <u>**BALANCED**</u>.

1) When a train or car or bus or anything else is <u>moving</u> at a <u>constant velocity</u> then the <u>forces</u> on it must all be <u>**BALANCED**</u>.
2) Never let yourself entertain the <u>ridiculous idea</u> that things need a constant overall force to <u>keep</u> them moving — NO NO NO NO NO NO!
3) To keep going at a <u>steady speed</u>, there must be <u>**ZERO RESULTANT FORCE**</u> — and don't you forget it.

Second Law — A Resultant Force Means Acceleration

If there is an <u>**UNBALANCED FORCE**</u>, then the object will <u>**ACCELERATE**</u> in that direction.

1) An <u>unbalanced</u> force will always produce <u>acceleration</u> (or deceleration).
2) This "<u>acceleration</u>" can take <u>**FIVE**</u> different forms:
   <u>Starting</u>, <u>stopping</u>, <u>speeding up</u>, <u>slowing down</u>, and <u>changing direction</u>.
3) On a force diagram, the <u>arrows</u> will be <u>unequal</u>:

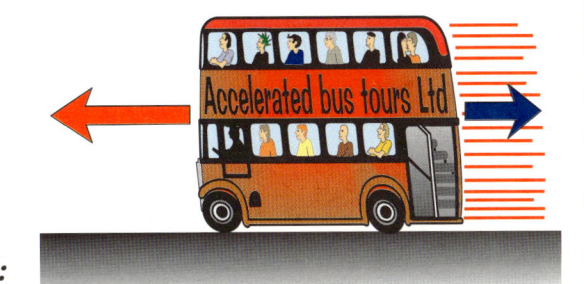

<u>Don't ever say</u>: "If something's moving there must be an overall resultant force acting on it".

Not so. If there's an <u>overall</u> force it will always <u>accelerate</u>. You get <u>steady</u> speed from <u>balanced</u> forces. I wonder how many times I need to say that same thing before you remember it?

Three Points That Should Be Obvious:

1) The bigger the <u>force</u>, the <u>GREATER</u> the <u>acceleration</u> or <u>deceleration</u>.
2) The bigger the <u>mass</u>, the <u>SMALLER</u> the <u>acceleration</u>.
3) To get a <u>big</u> mass to accelerate <u>as fast</u> as a <u>small</u> mass, it needs a <u>bigger</u> force.
   Just think about pushing <u>heavy</u> trolleys and it should all seem <u>fairly obvious</u>, I would hope.

Laws of motion? Repeal them at once — it's an outrage...

There's quite a few points on this page, and you really need to know them all — those laws of motion are pretty fundamental stuff. Just take each of the laws at a time, read through the points, <u>cover them up</u>, and try to <u>reproduce them</u>. Perfect material for <u>mini-essays</u>, I'd say.

SECTION TWO — FORCES AND MOTION

SEG Syllabus

Resultant Forces

Force and Acceleration

The Overall Unbalanced Force Is Often Called the Resultant Force

Any resultant force will produce acceleration, and this is the formula for it:

$$F = ma \quad \text{or} \quad a = F/m$$

m = mass, a = acceleration, F is always the RESULTANT FORCE.

Resultant Force Is Real Important — Especially for "F = ma"

The notion of RESULTANT FORCE is a real important one for you to get your head round. It's not especially tricky, it's just that it seems to get kind of ignored.

In most real situations there are at least two forces acting on an object along any direction. The overall effect of these forces will decide the motion of the object — whether it will accelerate, decelerate, or stay at a steady speed. The "overall effect" is found by just adding or subtracting the forces which point along the same direction. The overall force you get is called the RESULTANT FORCE.

And when you use the formula "F = ma", F must always be the RESULTANT FORCE.

Example 1

Q. What force is needed to accelerate a mass of 12kg at 5m/s² ?

ANS. The question is asking for force
— so you need a formula with "F = something-or-other".
Since they also give you values for mass and acceleration, the formula "F = ma" really should be a pretty obvious choice, surely.
So just stick in the numbers they give you where the letters are:
m = 12, a = 5, so "F = ma" gives F = 12 × 5 = 60N
(It's newtons because force always is).
(Notice that you don't really need to fully understand what's going on — you just need to know how to use formulae).

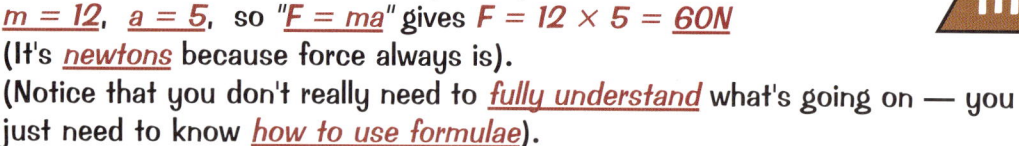

Example 2

EXAMPLE: A car of mass of 1,750kg has an engine which provides a driving force of 5,200N. At 70mph the drag force acting on the car is 5,150N.
Find its acceleration a) when first setting off from rest b) at 70mph.

ANSWER: 1) First draw a force diagram for both cases (no need to show the vertical forces):

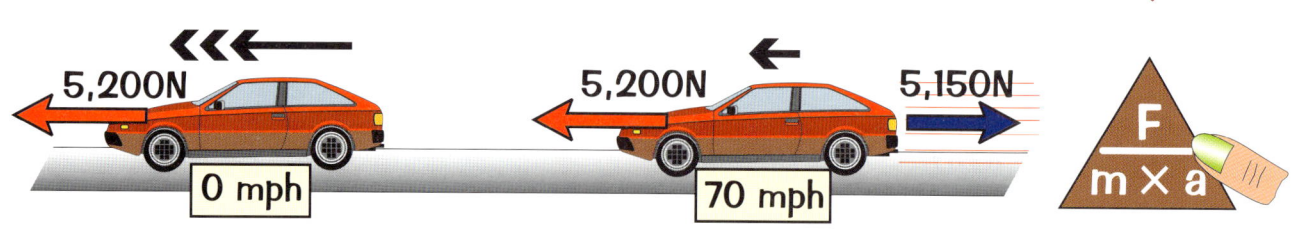

2) Work out the resultant force in each case, and apply "F = ma" using the formula triangle:

Resultant force = 5,200N
a = F/m = 5,200 ÷ 1,750 = **3.0 m/s²**

Resultant force = 5,200 − 5,150 = 50N
a = F/m = 50 ÷ 1750 = **0.03 m/s²**

Hey, did you know — an unbalanced force causes ac...

Make sure you fully understand what's happening in each of the calculations above. As with all calculations, the key to the stuff on this page is practice. There's simply no substitute...

SEG Syllabus

SECTION TWO — FORCES AND MOTION

Reaction Forces and Friction

Force and Acceleration

The Third Law — *Reaction Forces*

If object A *EXERTS A FORCE* on object B, then object B exerts *THE EXACT OPPOSITE FORCE* on object A.

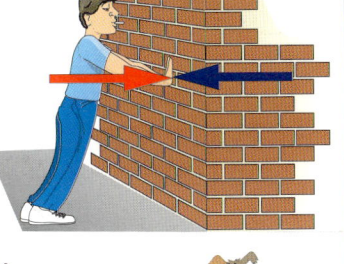

1) That means if you <u>push</u> against a wall, the wall will <u>push back</u> against you, <u>just as hard</u>.
2) And as soon as you <u>stop</u> pushing, <u>so does the wall</u>. Kinda clever really.
3) If you think about it, there must be an <u>opposing force</u> when you lean against a wall — otherwise you (and the wall) would <u>fall over</u>. 
4) If you <u>pull</u> a cart, whatever force <u>you exert</u> on the rope, the rope exerts on <u>you</u>. 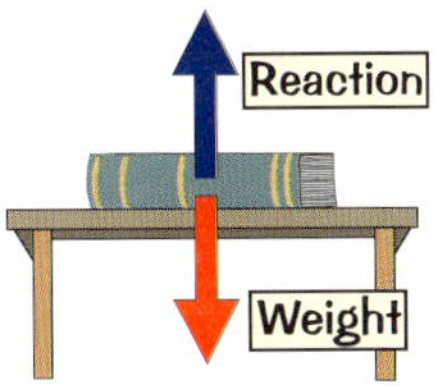
5) If you put a book on a table, the <u>weight</u> of the book acts <u>downwards</u> on the table — and the table exerts an <u>equal and opposite</u> force <u>upwards</u> on the book.
6) If you support a book on your <u>hand</u>, the book exerts its <u>weight</u> downwards on you, and you provide an <u>upwards</u> force on the book and it all stays nicely <u>in balance</u>.

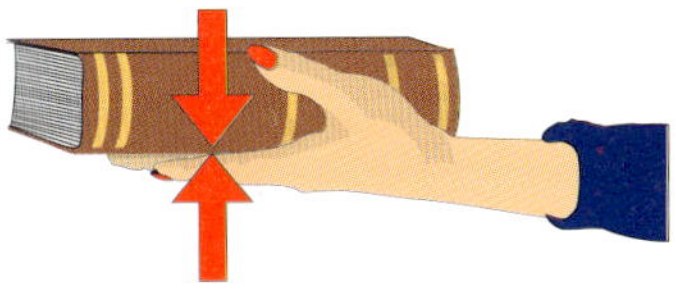

In <u>Exam</u> questions they may well <u>test</u> this by getting you to fill in some <u>extra arrow</u> to represent the <u>reaction force</u>. Learn this <u>very important fact</u>:

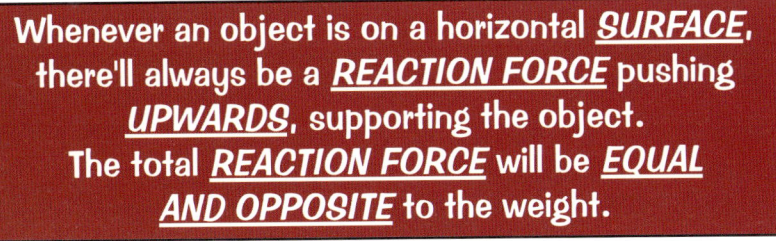

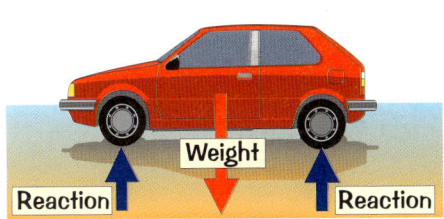

Whenever an object is on a horizontal *SURFACE*, there'll always be a *REACTION FORCE* pushing *UPWARDS*, supporting the object. The total *REACTION FORCE* will be *EQUAL AND OPPOSITE* to the weight.

Friction Is Always There to *Slow Things Down*

1) If an object has <u>no force</u> propelling it along it will always <u>slow down and stop</u> because of <u>friction</u>.
2) Friction always acts in the <u>opposite</u> direction to movement.
3) To travel at a <u>steady</u> speed, the driving force needs to <u>balance</u> the frictional forces.

Two Examples You Need to *Know*:

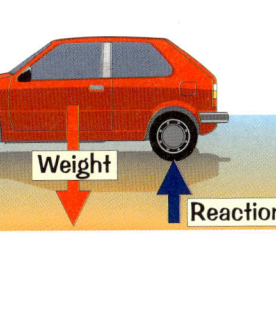

1) Friction between <u>solid surfaces</u> that are <u>gripping</u>. Acting between the a <u>tyre</u> and the <u>road</u>, this is the force that allows a car to corner (pretty handy, really). 
2) <u>Air resistance</u>. This <u>increases as the speed increases</u> — so a faster car will have to do more work to accelerate a given amount. And the final speed of a falling object will depend on its air resistance (see P. 28 on the <u>parachute</u>).

Learning about air resistance — it can be a real drag...

It looks like mini-essay time to me. There's a lot of details swirling around here, so definitely the best way of checking how much you know is to <u>scribble down a mini-essay</u> for each of the sections. Then <u>check back</u> and see what you <u>missed</u>. Then try again. <u>And keep trying</u>.

SECTION TWO — FORCES AND MOTION   SEG SYLLABUS

Stopping Distances for Cars

Force and Acceleration

They're pretty keen on this for Exam questions, so make sure you *learn it properly*.

The Many Factors That Affect Your Total Stopping Distance

The distance it takes to stop a car is divided into the THINKING DISTANCE and the BRAKING DISTANCE.

1) Thinking Distance

"The distance the car travels in the split-second between a hazard appearing and the driver applying the brakes".

It's affected by THREE MAIN FACTORS:

a) **How FAST you're going** — obviously. Whatever your reaction time, the *faster* you're going, the *further* you'll go.

b) **How DOPEY you are** — This is affected by *tiredness*, *drugs*, *alcohol*, *old-age*, and a *careless* blasé attitude.

c) **How BAD the VISIBILITY is** — lashing rain and oncoming lights, etc. make *hazards* harder to spot.

The figures below for typical stopping distances are from the Highway code. It's frightening to see just how far it takes to stop when you're going at 70mph.

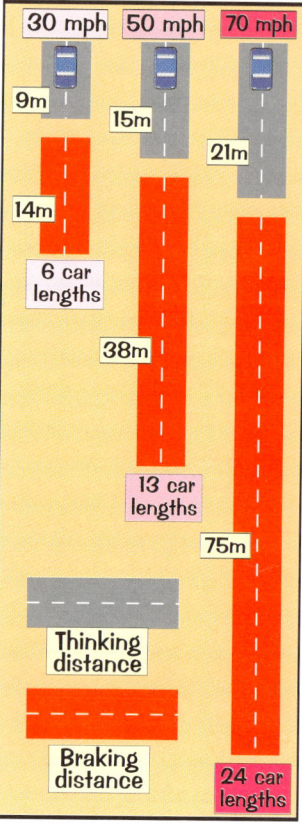

- 30 mph: 9m thinking + 14m braking = 6 car lengths
- 50 mph: 15m thinking + 38m braking = 13 car lengths
- 70 mph: 21m thinking + 75m braking = 24 car lengths

2) Braking Distance

"The distance the car travels during its deceleration whilst the brakes are being applied."

It's affected by FOUR MAIN FACTORS:

a) **How FAST you're going** — obviously. The *faster* you're going, the *further* it takes to stop (see below).

b) **How HEAVILY LOADED the vehicle is** — with the *same* brakes, *a heavily-laden* vehicle takes *longer to stop*. A car won't stop as quick when it's full of people and luggage and towing a caravan.

c) **How good your BRAKES are** — all brakes must be checked and maintained *regularly*. Worn or faulty brakes will let you down *catastrophically* just when you need them the *most*, i.e. in an *emergency*.

d) **How good the GRIP is** — this depends on THREE THINGS:
1) *road surface*, 2) *weather* conditions, 3) *tyres*.

Leaves and diesel spills and muck on t'road are *serious hazards* because they're *unexpected*. *Wet* or *icy roads* are always much more *slippy* than dry roads, but often you only discover this when you try to *brake* hard! Tyres should have a minimum *tread depth* of *1.6mm*. This is essential for getting rid of the *water* in wet conditions. Without *tread*, a tyre will simply *ride* on a *layer of water* and skid *very easily*. This is called "*aquaplaning*" and isn't nearly as cool as it sounds.

Stopping Distances Increase Alarmingly with Extra Speed

— Mainly Because of the v^2 Bit in KE=½mv²

To stop a car, the *kinetic energy*, ½mv², has to be *converted to heat energy* at the *brakes and tyres*: If you *double the speed*, you double the value of v, but the v^2 means that the *KE* is then increased by a factor of *four*. This means that you need *4 times* the *distance* to stop when applying the *maximum* possible braking force.

Muck on t'road, eh — by gum, it's grim up North...

They mention this specifically in the syllabus and are very likely to test you on it since it involves safety. Learn all the details and write yourself a *mini-essay* to see how much you *really know*.

Mass, Weight and Gravity

Force and Non-Uniform Motion

Gravity Is the Force of Attraction Between All Masses

Gravity attracts *all* masses, but you only notice it when one of the masses is *really really big*, e.g. a planet. Anything near a planet or star is *attracted* to it *very strongly*. This has *three* important effects:

1) It makes all things *accelerate* towards the *ground* (all with the *same* acceleration, *g*, which = $10m/s^2$ on Earth).
2) It gives everything a *weight*.
3) It keeps *planets*, *moons* and *satellites* in their *orbits*. The orbit is a *balance* between the *forward* motion of the object and the force of gravity pulling it *inwards*.

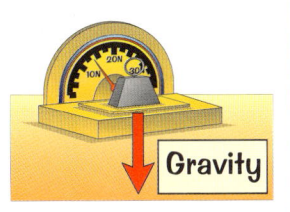

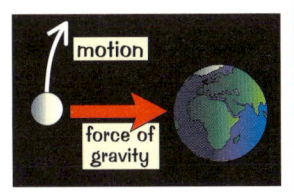

Weight and Mass Are Not the Same

To understand this you must *learn all these facts* about *mass and weight*:

1) *MASS* is the *AMOUNT OF MATTER* in an object. For any given object this will have the same value *ANYWHERE* in the Universe.
2) *WEIGHT* is caused by the *pull* of gravity. In most questions the *weight* of an object is just the *force* of gravity pulling it towards the centre of the *Earth*.
3) An object has the *same* mass whether it's on *Earth* or on the *Moon* — but its *weight* will be *different*. A 1 kg mass will *weigh LESS* on the Moon (1.6N) than it does on *Earth* (10N), simply because the *force* of gravity pulling on it is *less*.
4) Weight is a *force* measured in *newtons*. It must be measured using a *spring* balance or *newton meter*. MASS is *NOT* a force. It's measured in *kilograms* with a *mass* balance (never a spring balance).
5) One very fancy definition of a *newton*:

ONE NEWTON is the force needed to give a **MASS OF 1 kg** an **ACCELERATION OF $1m/s^2$**

The Very Important Formula Relating Mass, Weight and Gravity

$$W = m \times g$$

(Weight = mass × g)

1) Remember, weight and mass are **NOT the same**. Mass is in *kg*, weight is in *newtons*.
2) The letter "*g*" represents the *strength* of the gravity and its value is *different* for *different planets*. *On Earth* g = 10 N/kg. *On the Moon*, where the gravity is weaker, g is just 1.6 N/kg.
3) This formula is *hideously easy* to use:

EXAMPLE: What is the weight, in newtons, of a 5kg mass, both on Earth and on the Moon?

Answer: "W = m × g". On Earth: W = 5 × 10 = **50N** (The weight of the 5kg mass is 50N).
On the Moon: W = 5 × 1.6 = **8N** (The weight of the 5kg mass is 8N).

See what I mean. Hideously easy — as long as you've learnt what all the letters mean.

Learn about gravity NOW — no point in "weighting" around...

Very often, the only way to "*understand*" something is to *learn all the facts about it*. That's certainly true here. "Understanding" the difference between mass and weight is no more than learning all those facts about them. When you've learnt all those facts, you'll understand it...

SECTION TWO — FORCES AND MOTION
SEG SYLLABUS

Terminal Velocity

Force and Non-Uniform Motion

Balanced and Unbalanced Forces

TAKE NOTE! To move with a *steady speed* the forces must be in *BALANCE*. If there is an *unbalanced force* then you get *ACCELERATION*, not steady speed. That's *rrrreal important*, so don't forget it.

1) You only get *acceleration* with an overall *resultant* (unbalanced) *force*.
2) The *bigger* this *unbalanced force*, the *greater* the *acceleration*.

1) Steady Velocity — All Forces in Balance!

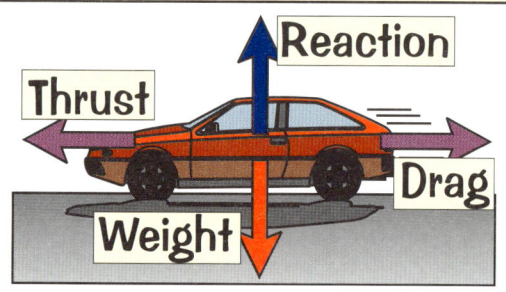

(Diagram: car with Thrust, Reaction, Drag, Weight)

2) Acceleration — Unbalanced Forces

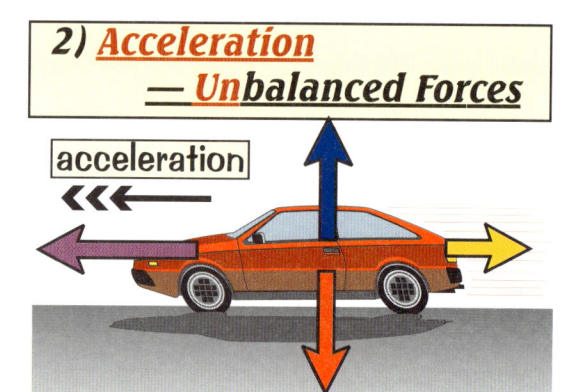

(Diagram: car with acceleration arrows)

Cars and Free-Fallers All Reach a Terminal Velocity

When cars and free-falling objects first *set off* they have *much more* force *accelerating* them than *resistance* slowing them down. As the *speed* increases the resistance *builds up*. This gradually *reduces* the *acceleration* until eventually the *resistance force* is *equal* to the *accelerating force* and then it won't be able to accelerate any more. It will have reached its maximum speed or *TERMINAL VELOCITY*.

(Graph: Velocity vs Time showing Maximum speed, or "terminal velocity")

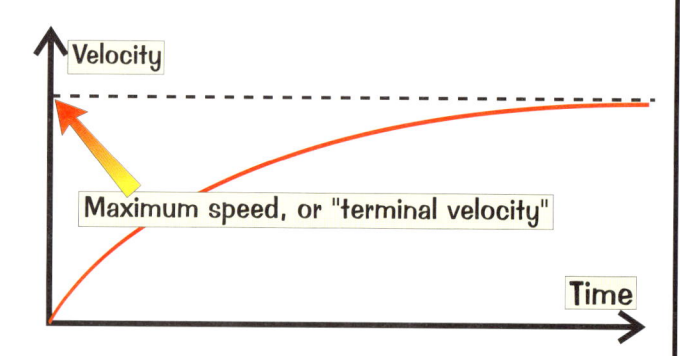

The Terminal Velocity of Falling Objects Depends on Their Shape and Area

The *accelerating force* acting on *all* falling objects is *GRAVITY*, and it would make them all fall at the *same* rate if it wasn't for *air resistance*. To prove this, on the Moon, where there's *no air*, hamsters and feathers dropped simultaneously will hit the ground *together*.
However, on Earth, *air resistance* causes things to fall at *different* speeds, and the *terminal velocity* of any object is determined by its *drag* in *comparison* to its *weight*. The drag depends on its *shape and area*.

The most important example is the human *skydiver*. Without his parachute open he has quite a *small* area and a force of "$W=mg$" pulling him down. He reaches a *terminal velocity* of about *120mph*.
But with the parachute *open*, there's much more *air resistance* (at any given speed) and still only the same force "$W=mg$" pulling him down. This means his *terminal velocity* comes right down to about *15mph*, which is a *safe speed* to hit the ground at.

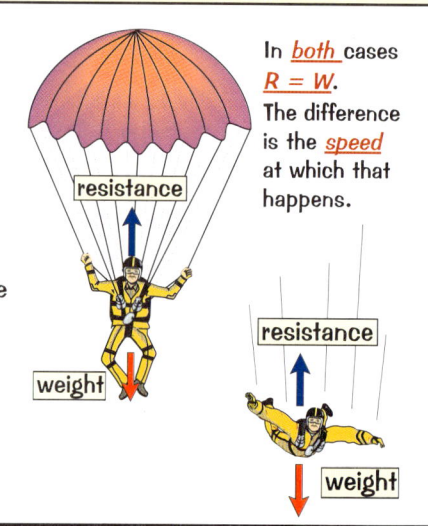

In *both* cases $R = W$. The difference is the *speed* at which that happens.

This really is terminally dreary stuff...

...But you've still got to know it. Make sure you can draw that graph for terminal velocity, and — more importantly — make sure you can explain it. And the same goes for balanced and unbalanced forces. It's pretty simple so long as you make the effort to *learn it*. So *scribble*...

SEG SYLLABUS

SECTION TWO — FORCES AND MOTION

Turning Forces

Force & Pressure on Solids, Liquids & Gases

A "Moment" Is a Turning Force

When a force acts on something that has a *pivot*, it creates a *turning force* called a *"moment"*. MOMENTS are *calculated* using this formula:

MOMENT = FORCE × PERPENDICULAR DISTANCE

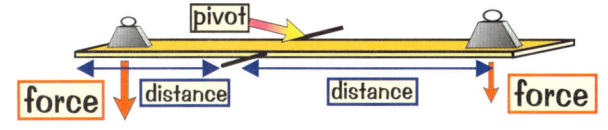

Also, for the system to be in *equilibrium*, (i.e. all *nicely balanced* and *not moving*) then *this must be true* too:

TOTAL CLOCKWISE MOMENT = TOTAL ANTICLOCKWISE MOMENT

Example:

Q: Bob just manages to move a boulder by pulling down with a force of *1,000N* on a *lever*, as shown in the diagram. What is the *force exerted on the boulder*?

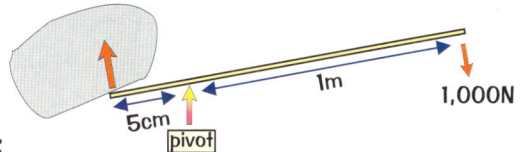

A: From the diagram, Bob's force is *1m from the pivot*, so:
TOTAL CLOCKWISE MOMENT = 1m × 1,000N = *1,000Nm*
This must *balance* the anticlockwise moment, so:
TOTAL ANTICLOCKWISE MOMENT = 1,000Nm = 0.05m × F
(Remember to *convert 5cm to m!*) So the force exerted on the boulder is:
F = 1,000Nm / 0.05m = *20,000 N*.
That's a pretty big force, I'd say. Now you know why levers are so handy...

Stretching, Compressing, Bending, Twisting, Shearing...

When a *combination of forces* are applied to a *solid object*, they can cause a *variety of effects*. You need to learn the diagrams below well enough to be able to put in all the details for each:

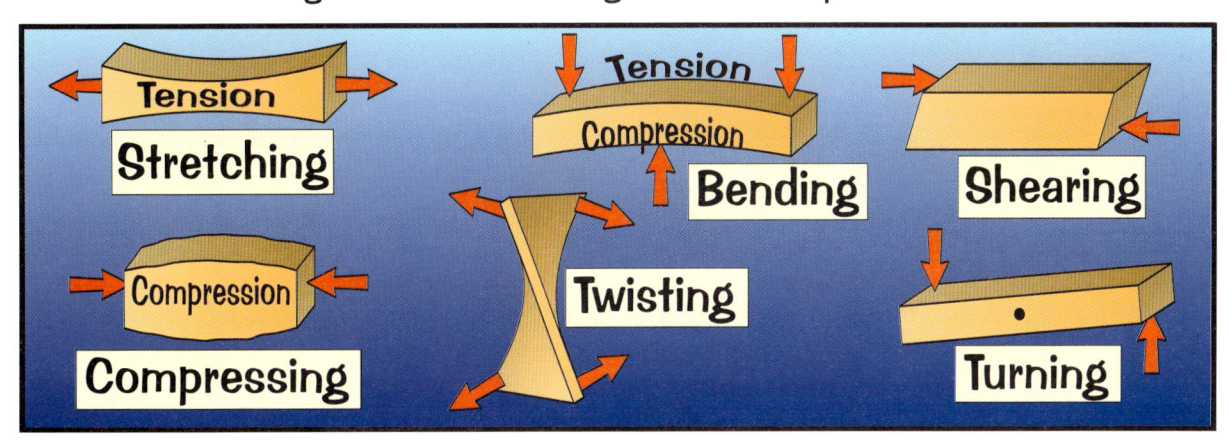

- **Stretching** — Tension
- **Compressing** — Compression
- **Bending** — Tension / Compression
- **Twisting**
- **Shearing**
- **Turning**

Make sure you can put in *all the forces* in all the *right places* and also identify in each case the places where the solid is under *tension* or *compression*. Note that sometimes an object does *not return* to its *original shape* when the forces are removed. This is known as *INELASTIC BEHAVIOUR*. (*Hooke's Law* applies to stretched objects — see P. 30).

What's a turning force called? Just a moment...

I would never have thought there were so many different forces. Well, you learn something new every day, and today it just happens to be turning forces. Make sure you can do those calculations — they can be a bit tricky I know, but the only way to get better is to *practise*...

SECTION TWO — FORCES AND MOTION
SEG SYLLABUS

Hooke's Law

Force & Pressure on Solids, Liquids & Gases

Stretching Springs — Extension Is Proportional to Load

This is *seriously easy*. It just means:

> If you **STRETCH** something with a **STEADILY INCREASING FORCE**, then the **LENGTH** will **INCREASE STEADILY** too.

The important thing to measure in a stretching experiment is not so much the total length as the **EXTENSION**;

> **EXTENSION** is the **INCREASE IN LENGTH** compared to the original length with *no force applied*.

For most materials, you'll find that **THE EXTENSION IS PROPORTIONAL TO THE LOAD**, which just means that if you *double* the load, the *extension will double too*.

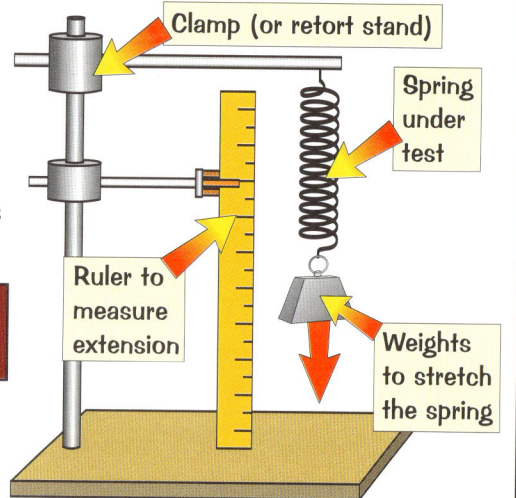

The Behaviour of the Spring Changes at the Elastic Limit:

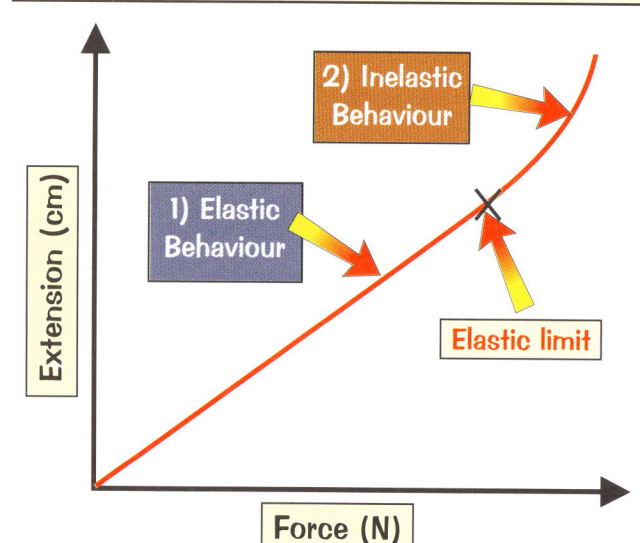

Region 1 — Elastic behaviour

1) In this region, when the load is *doubled* the extension *doubles too*.
2) The spring will *always return* to its original *size and shape* when the load is removed.

The Elastic Limit

1) The *elastic limit*. This is the point at which the behaviour of the spring suddenly changes.
2) *Below* this point the spring *keeps* its original *size and shape*.
3) *Above* this point the spring behaves *inelastically*.

If you put *too much* load on the spring then it will be *permanently damaged*.

Region 2 — Inelastic behaviour

1) In this region the spring *doesn't return* to its original *size and shape* when the load is *removed*.
2) The extension no longer doubles when the load is doubled.

You should **LEARN** that *elastic behaviour* always gives *A STRAIGHT LINE GRAPH THROUGH THE ORIGIN*.

Stretching springs — always loads of fun...

This is pretty standard stuff, so make sure you know all the little details, including the graph. You'd better be able to describe what happens in each region, and say exactly what the elastic limit is. Once you think you know it all, you know what to do: *cover, scribble, check, etc.*

SEG Syllabus   SECTION TWO — FORCES AND MOTION

Pressure on Surfaces

Force & Pressure on Solids, Liquids & Gases

Pressure Is *Not the Same* as Force

Too many people get *force* and *pressure* mixed up — but there's a *pretty serious difference* between them.

PRESSURE is defined as the FORCE ACTING on UNIT AREA of a surface.

Now read on, learn, and squirm with pleasure as another great mystery of the Physical Universe is exposed to your numb and weary mind...

Force Vs Pressure Has a Lot to Do with Damaging Surfaces

A force concentrated in a *small area* creates a *high pressure* — which means that the thing will *sink* into the surface. But with a *big* area, you get a *low* pressure which means it *doesn't* sink into the surface.

A Force Spread over a Big Area Means Low Pressure and No Sinking

Foundations   Snow shoes and skis    Tractor tyres    Drawing pins

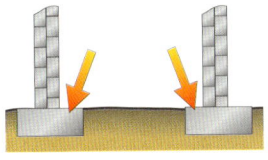

A Force Concentrated on a Small Area Means High Pressure and Damage

Ice skates   Stiletto heels   Sharp knives   Drawing pins

Pressure in Liquids Acts in All Directions and Increases with Depth

1) In a *gas* or *liquid* the same pressure acts outwards in *all* directions. This is *different* from solids, which transmit forces in *one direction only*.
2) Also, the *pressure* in a liquid or gas *increases* as you go *deeper*. This is due to the *weight* of all the stuff *above it* pushing down. Imagine the weight of all the water *directly* over you at a depth of 100m. All of that is *pushing down* on the water below and *increasing the pressure* down there. This is what *limits* the depth that submarines can reach before the pressure *crushes* the hull or bursts through a weak join somewhere.
3) The *increase* in pressure also depends on the *density* of the fluid. Air is *not very dense*, so air pressure changes *relatively little* as you go up through the atmosphere. Water *is* pretty dense though, so the pressure increases very quickly as you go *deeper*.

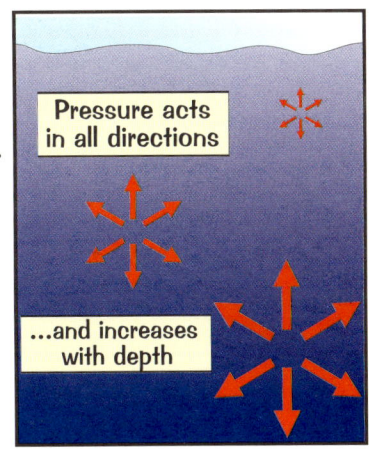

Pressure acts in all directions

...and increases with depth

Spread the load and reduce the pressure — start revising now...

It's funny old stuff is pressure. Force is a nice easy concept and people usually do fine with it. But pressure is just that bit trickier — and that means it can cause people a lot of gyp. Make sure you *learn all these details* about pressure. They're all worth marks in the Exam.

SECTION TWO — FORCES AND MOTION   SEG SYLLABUS

Pressure = Force / Area

Force & Pressure on Solids, Liquids & Gases

Pressure = Force / Area

The normal _unit of pressure_ is the _pascal_, Pa, which is the same as N/m². There is a fancy definition of the pascal. If you think it helps, you can learn it:

A pressure of ONE PASCAL is exerted by a FORCE OF 1N acting at right angles to an AREA of 1m²

They may well give you questions with areas given in _cm²_. Don't try to _convert cm² to m²_, which is a bit tricky. Instead, just work out the pressure using P = F/A in the normal way, but give the answer as N/cm² rather than N/m² (Pa). Do remember that N/cm² is _not_ the same as pascals (which are N/m²).

Hydraulics — the Main Application of "P = F/A"

Hydraulic systems all use _two important features_ of _pressure in liquids_. **LEARN THEM**:

1) **PRESSURE IS _TRANSMITTED THROUGHOUT THE LIQUID_**, so that the force can easily be applied _WHEREVER YOU WANT IT_, using flexible pipes.
2) The force can be _MULTIPLIED_ according to the _AREAS_ of the pistons used.

Hydraulic Jack

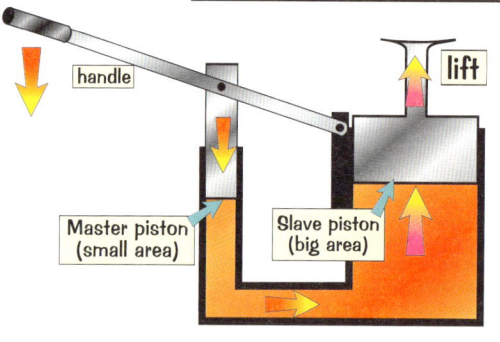

Car Brakes

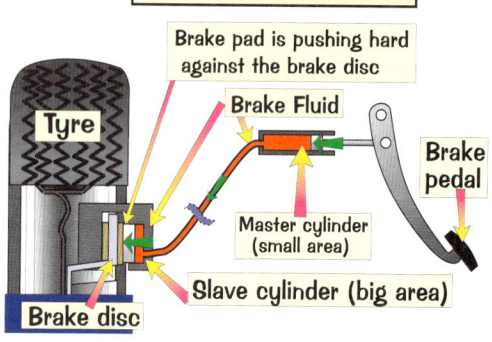

1) All hydraulic systems use a _SMALL master piston_ and a _BIG slave piston_.
2) The _master piston_ is used to apply a _force_, which puts the liquid _under pressure_.
3) This pressure is _transmitted_ throughout _all_ the liquid in the system, and somewhere _at the other end_ it pushes on the _slave piston_, which _exerts a force_ where it's needed.
4) The _slave piston_ always has a _much larger area_ than the _master piston_ so that it exerts a _much greater force_ from the pressure created by the force on the master piston. Clever stuff.
5) In this way, _hydraulic systems_ are _force multipliers_. i.e., they use a _small force_ to create a _very big force_ — a nice trick if you can do it.

The Typical Method for the Typical Exam Question:

1) Use the _master cylinder area_ and _force_ to calculate _THE PRESSURE IN THE SYSTEM_, P = F/A
2) Apply this pressure to the _area of the slave piston_ to calculate the _FORCE EXERTED_, F = P×A

EXAMPLE: The car master piston has an area of 4cm². If a force of 400N is applied to it, calculate the pressure created in the brake pipes. If the slave piston has an area of 40cm², calculate the force exerted on the brake disc.

ANSWER: At the _master piston_: Pressure created = F/A = 400N ÷ 4cm² = 100N/cm²   (not pascals!)
At the _slave piston_: Force produced = P×A = 100×40 = 4,000   (10 times original force)

Learn about hydraulics — and make light work of it...

You certainly need to know that formula for pressure, but that's pretty easy. The really tricky bit that you need to concentrate most on is how the formula is applied (twice) to explain how hydraulic systems turn a small force into a big one. _Keep working at it till you understand it._

SEG Syllabus   SECTION TWO — FORCES AND MOTION

Pressure in Gases

Force & Pressure on Solids, Liquids & Gases

Volume Is Inversely Proportional to Pressure

This sounds a lot more confusing than it actually is. Here is the fancy definition:

> When the PRESSURE IS INCREASED on a fixed mass of gas kept at constant temperature, the VOLUME WILL DECREASE. The changes in pressure and volume are in INVERSE PROPORTION.

If you ask me it's a pretty obvious way for a gas to behave. In simple language it's just this:

> If you squash a gas into a smaller space, the pressure goes up in proportion to how much you squash it. e.g. if you squash it to half the amount of space, it'll end up at twice the pressure it was before (so long as you don't let it get hotter or colder, or let any escape). Simple, innit?

It can work the other way too. If you increase the PRESSURE, the volume must DECREASE. If you increase the VOLUME, the pressure must DECREASE. That's all pretty obvious though isn't it?

Gas Syringe Experiments Are Good for Showing This Law

1) A gas syringe makes a pretty good airtight seal and is great for demonstrating this law.

2) You put weights on the top to give a definite known force pushing down on the piston.

3) If you double the weight, you also double the force, which doubles the pressure.

4) You can then measure the volume change using the scale on the side of the syringe. Easy peasy.

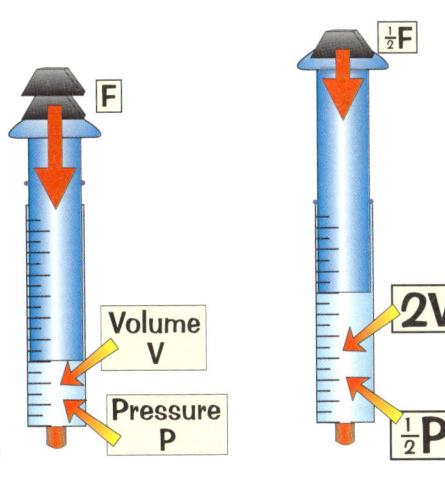

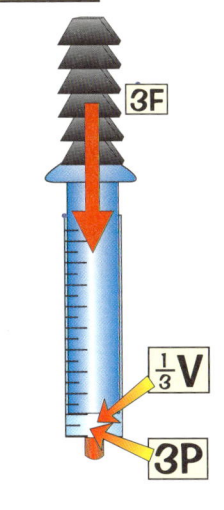

Using the Formula "$P_1V_1 = P_2V_2$"

Well what can I say, it's another formula. Not quite one you can put in a triangle, but still the same old idea: stick in the numbers they give you, and work out the value for the remaining letter. Please try and get it into your head that you don't need to fully understand the Physics, you just need a bit of "common sense" about formulae. Understanding always helps of course, but you can still get the right answer without it! Really, you've just got to identify the values for each letter — the rest is very routine.

EXAMPLE: A gas is compressed from a volume of 300cm³ at a pressure of 2.5 atmospheres down to a volume of 175cm³. Find the new pressure, in atmospheres.

ANSWER: "$P_1V_1 = P_2V_2$" gives: $2.5 \times 300 = P_2 \times 175$, so $P_2 = (2.5 \times 300) \div 175 = 4.3$ atm.

N.B. For this formula, always keep the units the same as they give them (in this case, pressure in atmospheres).

Less space, more collisions, more pressure — just like London...

This is another topic that can seem a lot more confusing than it really is. The basic principle of the law is simple enough, and so is the Gas Syringe demo. The formula might look bad but really there's nothing to it. In the end it's just stuff that needs learning, that's all. Scribble.

SECTION TWO — FORCES AND MOTION   SEG SYLLABUS

Revision Summary for Section Two

More jolly questions that I know you're going to really enjoy. There are lots of bits and bobs on forces, motion and pressure that you definitely need to know. Some bits are certainly quite tricky to understand, but there's also loads of straightforward stuff that just needs to be learnt, ready for instant regurgitation in the Exam. You have to practise these questions over and over and over again, until you can answer them all really easily — phew, such jolly fun.

1) What's the difference between speed and velocity? Give an example of each.
2) Write down the formula for working out speed. Find the speed of a partly chewed mouse that hobbles 3.2m in 35s. Find how far it would get in 25 minutes.
3) Sketch a typical distance-time graph and point out all the important parts of it.
4) Write down four important points (seven for higher level) relating to this graph.
5) Explain how to calculate velocity from a distance-time graph.
6) What's acceleration? Is it the same thing as speed or velocity? What are its units?
7) Write down the formula for acceleration. What's the acceleration of a soggy pea, flicked from rest to a speed of 14 m/s in 0.4s?
8) Write down the First Law of Motion. Illustrate with a diagram.
9) Write down the Second Law of Motion. Illustrate with a diagram. What's the formula for it?
10) Explain what "resultant force" is. Illustrate with a diagram. When do you most need it?
11) A force of 30N pushes on a trolley of mass 4kg. What is its acceleration?
12) What's the mass of a cat that accelerates at 9.8 m/s^2 when acted on by a force of 56N?
13) Write down the Third Law of Motion. Illustrate it with four diagrams.
14) Explain what reaction force is and where it pops up. Is it important to know about it?
15) Explain what friction is, and name two different types. Give an example for each.
16) What are the two different parts of the overall stopping distance of a car?
17) List the three or four factors that affect each of the two sections of stopping distance.
18) Which formula explains why the stopping distance increases so much? Explain why it does.
19) What is gravity? List the three main effects that gravity produces.
20) Explain the difference between mass and weight. What units are they measured in?
21) What's the formula for weight? Illustrate it with a worked example of your own.
22) What is "terminal velocity"? Is it the same thing as maximum speed?
23) What are the two main factors affecting the terminal velocity of a falling object?
24) What is the name given to a turning force? Give its formula.
25) What condition must be met for turning forces to be in equilibrium?
26) List the six different kinds of force. Sketch diagrams to illustrate them all.
27) What is Hooke's Law? Sketch the usual apparatus. Explain what you must measure.
28) Explain the differences between "elastic" and "inelastic" behaviour.
29) What's the definition of pressure? What combination of force and area gives high pressure?
30) What happens to pressure as you go deeper? Which direction does the pressure act in?
31) What's the formula for pressure? What units is pressure given in? What's the definition?
32) Write down the two features of pressure in liquids that allow hydraulic systems to work.
33) Sketch a jack and a car braking system and explain how they work as force multipliers.
34) What is the pressure law? Sketch an experiment that demonstrates it. What's the formula?
35) A fixed amount of gas at 5,000 Pa is compressed down to 60cm^3, and in the process its pressure rises to 260,000 Pa. What was the volume before it got compressed?

SEG Syllabus

WAVES

Waves — Basic Principles
Characteristics of Waves

Waves are different from anything else. They have various features which *only waves have*:

Amplitude, Wavelength and Frequency

Too many people get these *wrong*. Take careful note:
1) The AMPLITUDE goes from the *middle* line to the *peak*, NOT from a trough to a peak.
2) The WAVELENGTH covers a *full cycle* of the wave, e.g. from *peak to peak*, not just from "*two bits that are sort of separated a bit*".
3) FREQUENCY is how many *complete waves* there are *per second* (passing a certain point).

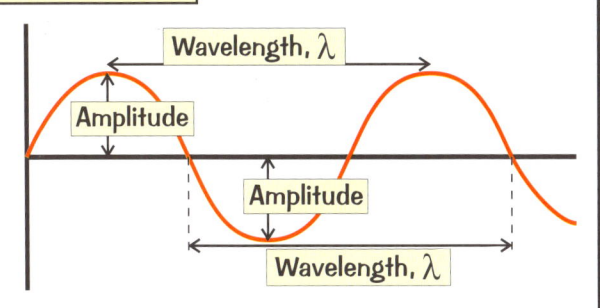

Transverse Waves Have Sideways Vibrations

Most waves are TRANSVERSE:
1) *Light* and all other *EM radiation*.
2) *Ripples* on water.
3) *Waves* on *strings*.
4) A *slinky spring* wiggled from side to side (or up and down).

In *TRANSVERSE WAVES* the vibrations are at *90⁰* to the *direction of travel* of the wave.

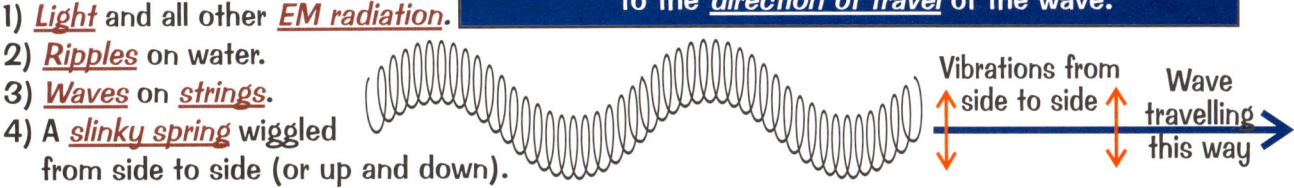

Longitudinal Waves Have Vibrations Along the Same Line

The ONLY longitudinal waves are:
1) *Sound*. It travels as a longitudinal wave through solids, liquids and gases.
2) *Shock waves* e.g. seismic *P-waves*.
3) A *slinky spring* when plucked.
4) *Don't get confused* by CRO displays, which show a *transverse wave* when displaying *sound*. The real wave is *longitudinal* — the display shows a transverse wave *just so you can see what's going on*.

In *LONGITUDINAL WAVES* the vibrations are *ALONG THE SAME DIRECTION* as the wave is travelling.

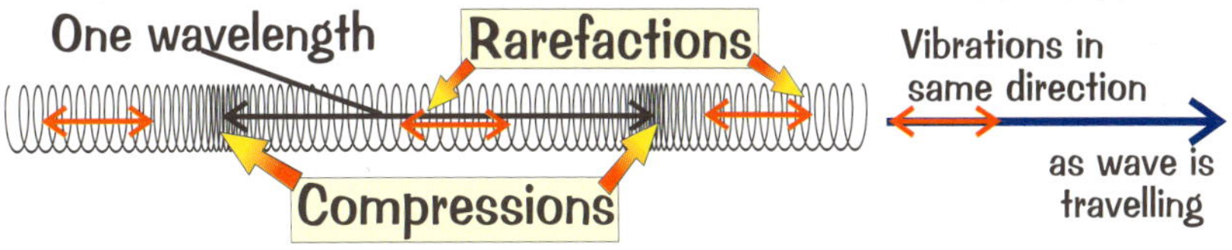

All Waves Carry Energy — Without Transferring Matter

1) *Light*, *infrared*, and *microwaves* all make things *warm up*. *X-rays* and *gamma rays* can cause *ionisation* and *damage* to cells, which also shows that they carry *energy*.
2) *Loud* sounds make things *vibrate or move*. Even the quietest sound moves your *ear drum*.
3) Waves on the sea can *toss big boats around* and can be used to generate *electricity*.

Waves Can Be REFLECTED and REFRACTED

1) They might test whether or not you realise these are *properties* of waves, so *learn them*.
2) The two words are *confusingly similar*, but you MUST learn the *differences* between them.
3) Light and sound are *reflected* and *refracted*, and this shows that they travel as waves.

Learn about waves — just get into the vibes, man...

This is all very basic stuff on waves. Five sections with some tasty titbits in each. *Learn* the headings, then the details. Then *cover the page* and see what you can *scribble down*. Then try again until you can remember the whole lot. It's all just *easy marks to be won... or lost*.

SECTION THREE — WAVES
SEG SYLLABUS

The Wave Equation

Characteristics of Waves

The speed of a wave is given by the formula $v = f\lambda$, or
WAVE SPEED (m/s) = FREQUENCY (Hz) x WAVELENGTH (m)
This is known as the **WAVE EQUATION**, and you've gotta know it.

If you think about it, it kinda makes sense. The *frequency* is just the *number of waves* emitted *each second*, and the *wavelength* is the *length* of the wave. All the waves are *end to end*, so the total length emitted each second must be $f\lambda$. Since these waves must get out of the way for the next lot, they will *move this distance each second* — and how much it moves each second is simply the *speed* of the wave.

The First Rule: Try and Choose the Right Formula

1) People have *way too much difficulty* deciding which *formula* to use.
2) All too often the question starts with *"A wave is travelling..."*, and in they leap with *"v = f\lambda"*.
3) To choose the *right formula* you have to look for the *THREE quantities* mentioned in the question.
4) If the question mentions *speed*, *frequency* and *wavelength* then sure, "$v = f\lambda$" is the one to use.
5) But if it has *speed*, *time* and *distance* then "$s = d/t$" is more the order of the day — *wouldn't you say*.

a) Some ripples travel 55cm in 5 seconds. Find their speed in cm/s.
   ANSWER: Speed, distance and time are mentioned in the question,
   so we must use "$s=d/t$": $s = d/t = 55/5 =$ **11cm/s**.
b) The wavelength of these waves is found to be 2.2cm. What is their frequency?
   ANSWER: This time we have f and λ mentioned, so we use "$v = f\lambda$", and we'll need this:
   It tells us that $f = v/\lambda = 11\text{cm/s} \div 2.2\text{cm} =$ **5Hz** (It's very cool to use cm/s with cm, s and Hz).

The Second Rule: Watch Those Units — the Little Rascals

1) The *standard (SI) units* involved with waves are: *metres*, *seconds*, *m/s* and *hertz* (Hz).

If you want your answer in SI units, always CONVERT INTO SI UNITS (m, s, Hz, m/s) before you work anything out.

2) The trouble is waves often have *high frequencies* given in *kHz* or *MHz*, so make sure you *learn this* too:

1 kHz (kilohertz) = 1,000 Hz   1 MHz (megahertz) = 1,000,000 Hz

3) *Wavelengths* can also be given in *funny* units, e.g. *km* for long wave radio, or *cm* for sound.
4) There's worse still: The *speed of light* is 3×10^8 m/s = *300,000,000 m/s*. This, along with numbers like *900MHz* = *900,000,000 Hz* won't fit into a lot of calculators. That leaves you *three* choices:

   1) Enter the numbers as *standard form* (3×10^8 and 9×10^8), or...
   2) *Cancel* three or six *noughts* off both numbers, (so long as you're *dividing* them!) or...
   3) Do it entirely *without* a calculator! (no really, I've seen it done).   Your choice.

Example 2 — Sound

Q) A sound wave travelling in a solid has a frequency of 19 kHz and a wavelength of 12cm. Find its speed.
ANSWER: We have f and λ mentioned, so we'll use "$v = f\lambda$". But we must convert the units into SI:
So, $v = f \times \lambda = 19{,}000\text{Hz} \times 0.12\text{m} =$ **2,280 m/s** — convert the units and there's *no problem*.

Example 3 — EM Radiation:

Q) A radio wave has a frequency of 92.2 MHz. Find its wavelength. (The speed of light is 3×10^8 m/s.)
ANSWER: We have f and λ mentioned, so we'll use "$v = f\lambda$". Radio waves travel at the speed of light, of course. Once again, we must convert the units into SI, but we'll also have to use standard form:
$\lambda = v/f = 3\times10^8 / 92{,}200{,}000 = 3\times10^8 / 9.22\times10^7 =$ **3.25m** (There's a few bits to get wrong).

This stuff on formulae is really painful — I mean it MHz...

Sift out the main rules on this page, then *cover it up* and *scribble them down*. Then try these:
1) A sound wave has a frequency of 2,500Hz and a wavelength of 13.2cm. Find its speed.
2) The radio waves for Radio 4 have a wavelength of 1.5 km. Find their frequency.

SEG SYLLABUS   SECTION THREE — WAVES

Reflection

Light

The Ripple Tank Is Really Good for Displaying Waves

Learn all these diagrams showing _reflection of waves_. They could ask you to complete _any one of them_ in the Exam. It can be quite a bit _trickier_ than you think unless you've _practised_ them real well _beforehand_.

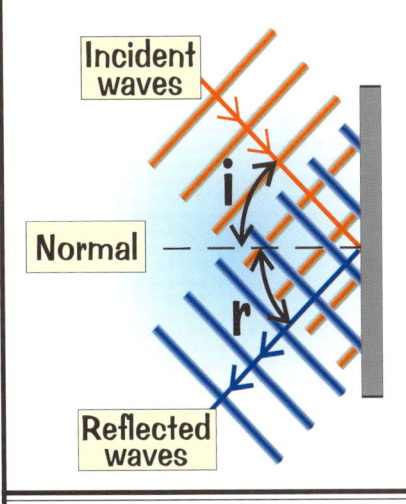

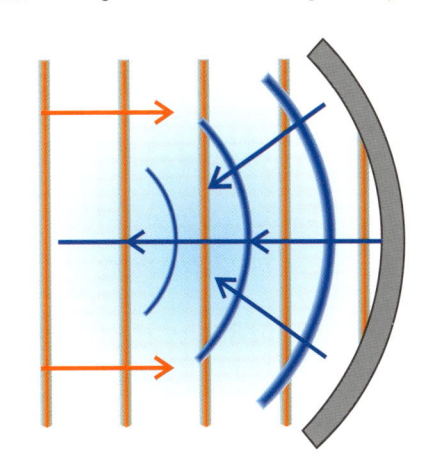

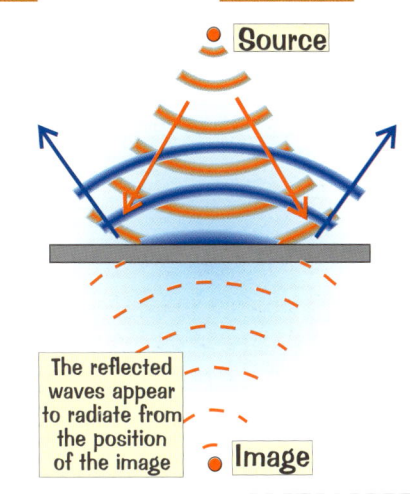

Reflection of Light

Reflection of light is what allows us to _SEE_ objects.
When light reflects from an _even_ surface (_smooth and shiny_ like a _mirror_) then it's all reflected at the _same angle_ and you get a _clear reflection_.
Sound also reflects off _hard surfaces_ in the form of _echoes_.
Reflection of light and of sound gives evidence that light and sound travel as waves.
And don't forget, THE LAW OF REFLECTION applies to _every reflected ray_:

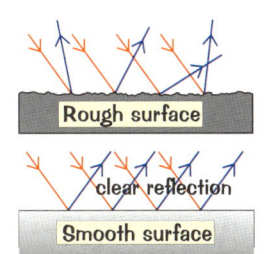

Angle of INCIDENCE = Angle of REFLECTION

Reflection in a Plane Mirror — How to Locate the Image

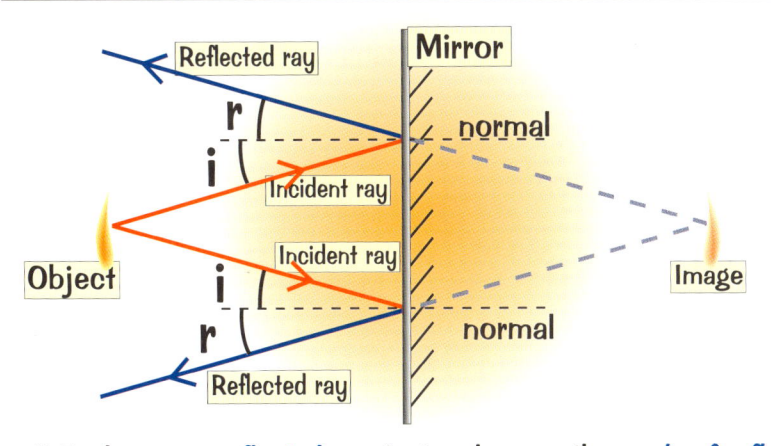

You need to be able to _reproduce_ this entire diagram of _how an image is formed_ in a PLANE MIRROR.
Learn these _two_ important points:

1) The _image_ is the _SAME SIZE_ as the _object_.
2) It is _AS FAR BEHIND_ the mirror as the object is _in front_.

1) To draw _any reflected ray_, just make sure the _angle of reflection_, r, equals the _angle of incidence_, i.
2) Note that these two angles are _ALWAYS_ defined between the ray itself and the dotted _NORMAL_.
3) _Don't ever_ label them as the angle between the ray and the _surface_. Definitely uncool.

Learn reflection thoroughly — try to look at it from all sides...

First make sure you can draw all those diagrams from memory. Then make sure you've learnt the rest well enough to answer typical meany Exam questions like these: "_Explain why you can see a piece of paper_" "_Why is the image in a plane mirror virtual?_"

SECTION THREE — WAVES

SEG SYLLABUS

Refraction

Light

Refraction is when waves change *direction* as they enter a *different medium*.

1) Refraction of Light — the Good Old Glass Block Demo

You can't fail to remember the old "*ray of light through a rectangular glass block*" trick. Make sure you can draw this diagram *from memory*, with every detail *perfect*.

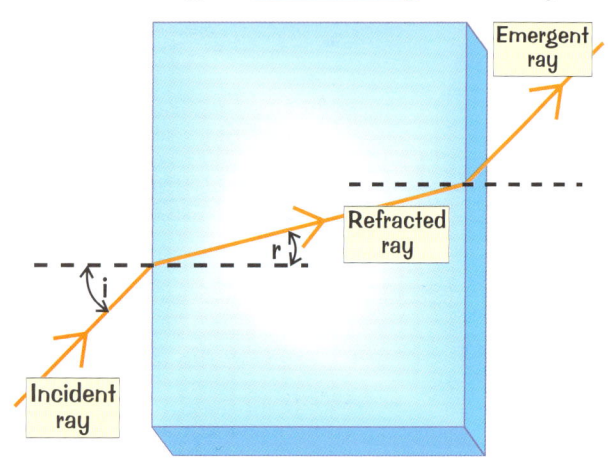

1) *Take careful note* of the positions of the *normals* and the *exact positions* of the angles of *incidence* and *refraction* (and note it's the angle of *refraction* — not *reflection*).
2) Most important of all remember *which way* the ray *bends*.
3) The ray bends *towards* the normal as it enters the *denser medium*, and *away* from the normal as it *emerges* into the *less dense* medium.
4) Try to *visualise* the shape of the *wiggle* in the diagram — that can be easier than remembering the rule in words.

2) Sound Also Refracts, but It's Hard to Spot

Sound will also refract (change direction) as it enters *different media*. However, since sound is always *spreading out so much*, the change in direction is *hard to spot* under normal circumstances. But just remember, *sound does refract*, OK? The fact that sound and light are both refracted gives *further evidence* that they travel as *waves*.

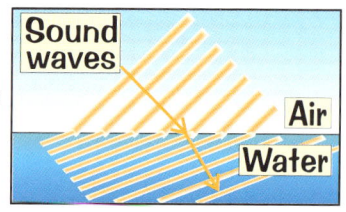

3) Refraction Is Always Caused by the Waves Changing Speed

1) When waves *slow down* they bend *towards* the normal.
2) When *light* enters *glass* it *slows down* to about *2/3* of its normal speed (in air) i.e. it slows down to about 2×10^8 m/s rather than 3×10^8 m/s.
3) When waves hit the boundary *along a normal*, i.e. at *exactly 90°*, then there will be *no change* in direction. That's pretty important to remember, because they often *sneak* it into a question somewhere. There'll still be a change in *speed* and *wavelength*, though.
4) *Some* light is also *reflected* when light hits a *different medium* such as glass.

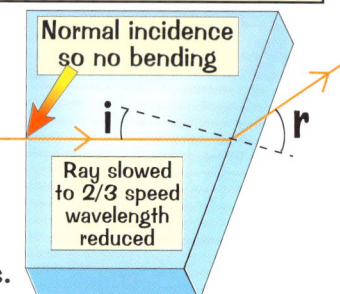

4) Refraction Is Shown by Waves in a Ripple Tank Slowing Down

1) The waves travel *slower* in *shallower water*, causing *refraction* as shown.
2) There's a change in *direction* and a change in *wavelength*, but *NO change* in *frequency*.

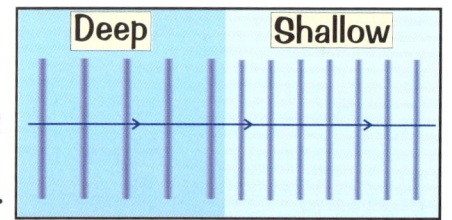

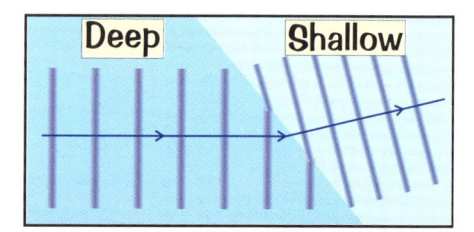

Revise refraction — but don't let it slow you down...

The first thing you've gotta do is make sure you can spot the difference between the words *refraction* and *reflection*. After that you need to *learn all this stuff about refraction* — so you know exactly what it is. Make sure you know all those *diagrams* inside out. *Cover and scribble*.

SEG Syllabus   SECTION THREE — WAVES

Refraction: Two Special Cases

Light

Dispersion Produces Rainbows

1) _Different colours_ of light are _refracted_ by _different amounts_.
2) This is because they travel at _slightly different speeds_ in any given _medium_.
3) A _prism_ can be used to make the different colours of white light emerge at _different angles_.
4) This produces a _spectrum_ showing all the colours of the _rainbow_. This effect is called DISPERSION.

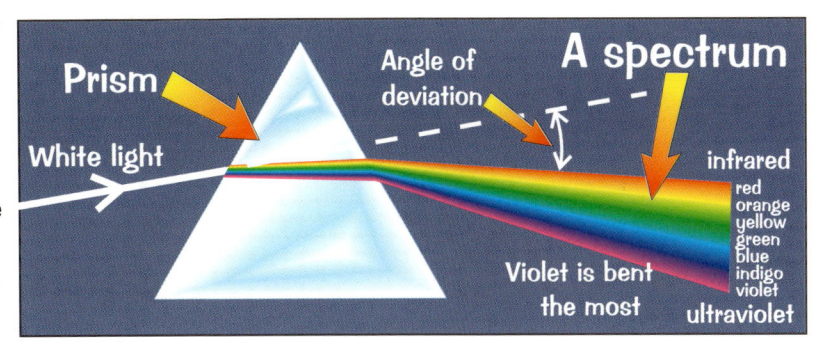

Prism — White light → Angle of deviation → A spectrum: infrared, red, orange, yellow, green, blue, indigo, violet, ultraviolet. Violet is bent the most.

5) You need to know that _red light_ is refracted the _least_ — and _violet_ is refracted the _most_.
6) Also know the _order_ of colours in between: Red Orange Yellow Green Blue Indigo Violet
   which is remembered by: Richard Of York Gave Battle In Velcro
   They may well test whether you can put them correctly into the diagram.
7) Also learn where _infrared_ and _ultraviolet_ light would appear if you could detect them.

Total Internal Reflection and the Critical Angle

1) This _only_ happens when _light_ is _coming out_ of something _dense_ like _glass_ or _water_ or _perspex_.
2) If the _angle_ is _shallow enough_ the ray _won't come out at all_, but it _reflects_ back into the glass (or whatever). This is called _total internal reflection_ because **ALL** of the light _reflects back in_.
3) You definitely need to learn this set of **THREE DIAGRAMS** that show the three conditions:

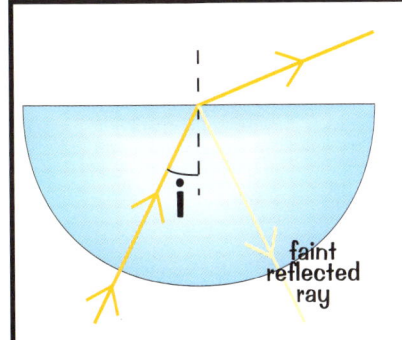

Angle of Incidence LESS than the Critical Angle.
Most of the light _passes through_ into the air but a _little_ bit of it is _internally reflected_.

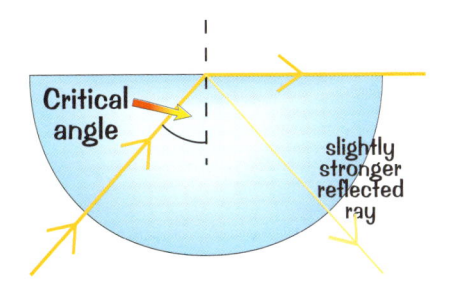

Angle of Incidence EQUAL TO the Critical Angle.
The emerging ray comes out _along the surface_. There's quite a bit of _internal reflection_.

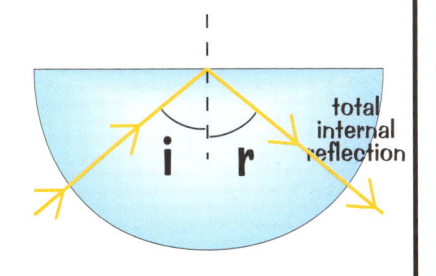

Angle of Incidence GREATER than the Critical Angle.
No light comes out. It's _all_ internally reflected, i.e. _total internal reflection_.

1) The _Critical Angle_ for _glass_ is about 42°. This is _very handy_ because it means _45° angles_ can be used to get _total internal reflection_ as in the _prisms_ in the _binoculars_ and _periscope_ shown on the next page.
2) In DIAMOND the _Critical Angle_ is much _lower_, about 24°. This is why diamonds _sparkle_ so much — there are lots of _internal reflections_.

Revision — sure it's critical, but it's not a prism sentence...

First and foremost make sure you can _scribble all the diagrams_ down with all the details. Then _scribble a mini-essay_ for each topic, jotting down everything you can remember. Then check back and see what you _missed_. Then _learn the stuff you forgot_ and _try again_. Ahh... such fun.

SECTION THREE — WAVES   SEG SYLLABUS

Total Internal Reflection

Light

Binoculars

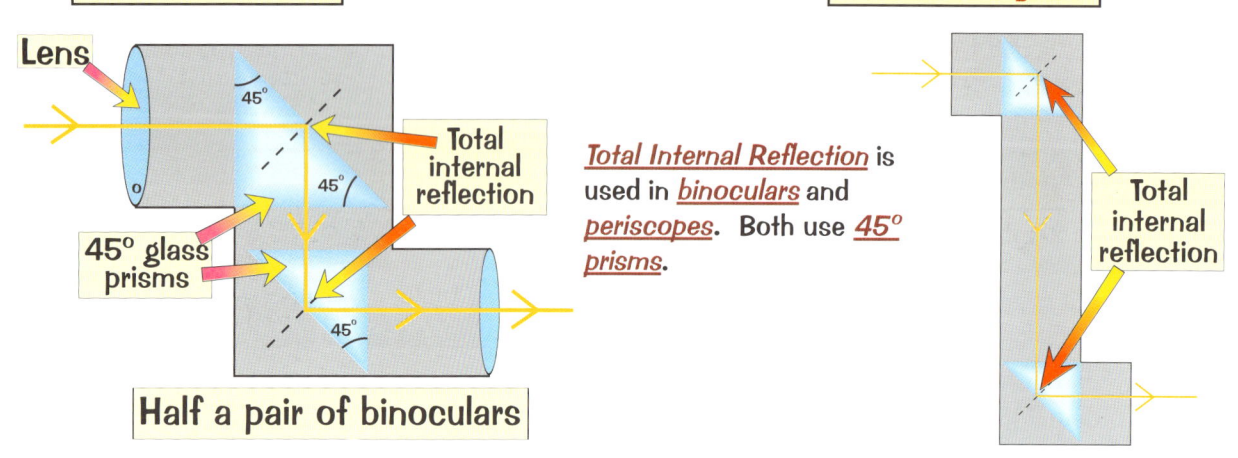

Half a pair of binoculars

Periscope

Total Internal Reflection is used in binoculars and periscopes. Both use 45° prisms.

Binoculars and the periscope use prisms because they give slightly better reflection than a mirror would, and they're also easier to hold accurately in place. Learn the exact positioning of the prisms. They could ask you to complete a diagram of a binocular or periscope and unless you've practised beforehand you'll find it pretty tricky to draw the prisms in properly.

Optical Fibres — Communications and Endoscopes

1) Optical fibres can carry information over long distances by repeated total internal reflections.
2) Optical communications have several advantages over electrical signals in wires:
   a) the signal doesn't need boosting as often.
   b) a cable of the same diameter can carry a lot more information.
   c) the signals cannot be tapped into, or suffer interference from electrical sources.
3) Normally no light whatever would be lost at each reflection. However some light is lost due to imperfections in the surface, so it still needs boosting every few km.

The fibre must be narrow enough to keep the angles below the critical angle, as shown, so the fibre mustn't be bent too sharply anywhere.

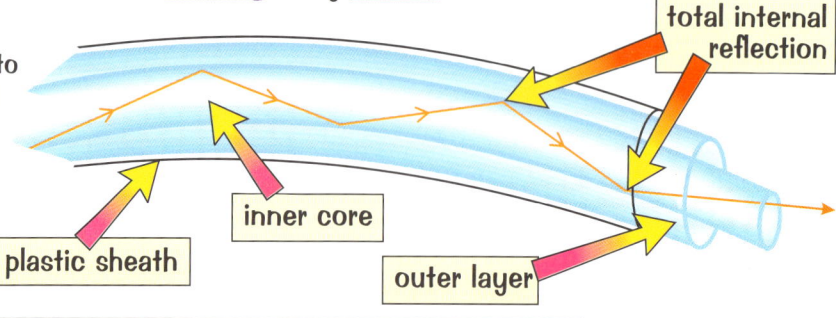

Endoscopes Are Used to Look Inside People

This is a narrow bunch of optical fibres with a lens system at each end. Another bunch of optical fibres carries light down inside to see with.
The image is displayed as a full colour moving image on a TV screen. Real impressive stuff. This means they can do operations without cutting big holes in people. This was never possible before optical fibres.

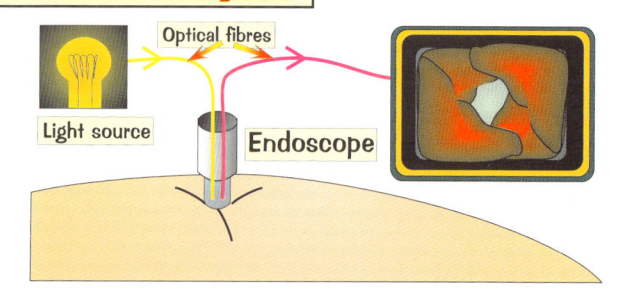

Total internal reflection — sounds like a government inquiry...

Three sections to learn here, with diagrams for each. They always have at least one of these applications of total internal reflection in the Exam. Learn them all. None of this is difficult — but just make sure you've got all those little picky details firmly fastened inside your head.

SEG SYLLABUS SECTION THREE — WAVES

Diffraction

Light

This word sounds a lot more technical than it really is.

Diffraction Is Just the "Spreading Out" of Waves

All waves tend to spread out at the edges when they pass through a gap or past an object. Instead of saying that the wave "spreads out" or "bends" round a corner, you should say that it DIFFRACTS around the corner. It's as easy as that. That's all diffraction means.

A Wave Spreads More if It Passes Through a Narrow Gap

The ripple tank shows this effect quite nicely. The same effect applies to light and sound too.

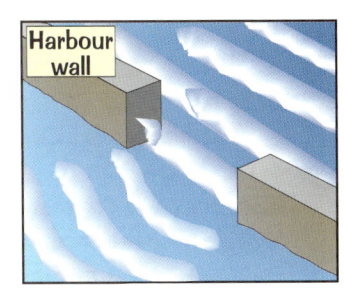

1) A "narrow" gap is one which is about the same size as the wavelength or less.
2) Obviously then, the question of whether a gap is "narrow" or not depends on the wave in question. What may be a narrow gap for a water wave will be a huge gap for a light wave.
3) It should be obvious then, that the longer the wavelength of a wave, the more it will diffract.

Sounds Always Diffract Quite a Lot, Because λ is Quite Big

1) Most sounds have wavelengths in air of around 0.1m, which is quite long.
2) This means they spread out round corners so you can still hear people even when you can't see them directly (the sound usually reflects off walls too which also helps).
3) Higher frequency sounds will have shorter wavelengths and so they won't diffract as much, which is why things sound more "muffled" when you hear them from round corners.

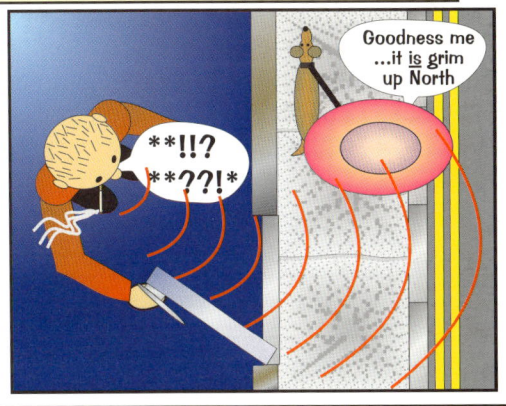

Long Wavelength Radio Waves Diffract Easily over Hills and into Buildings:

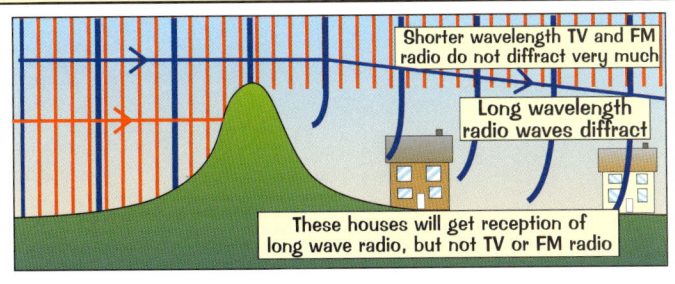

Visible Light on the Other Hand...

has a very short wavelength, and it'll only diffract with a very narrow slit:

This spreading or diffraction of light (and radio waves) is strong evidence for the wave nature of light.

Diffraction — it can drive you round the bend...

People usually don't know much about diffraction, mainly because there are so few lab demos you can do to show it, and there's also very little to say about it — about one page's worth, in fact. The thing is though, if you just learn this page properly, then you'll know all you need to.

SECTION THREE — WAVES

SEG SYLLABUS

The E.M. Spectrum

The Electromagnetic Spectrum

There Are Seven Basic Types of Electromagnetic Wave

We split Electromagnetic waves (EM waves) into _seven_ basic types as shown below.
These EM waves form a _continuous spectrum_ so the different regions do actually _merge_ into each other.

RADIO WAVES	MICRO- WAVES	INFRA- RED	VISIBLE LIGHT	ULTRA- VIOLET	X-RAYS	GAMMA RAYS
$1m-10^4 m$	$10^{-2}m$ (3cm)	$10^{-5}m$ (0.01mm)	$10^{-7}m$	$10^{-8}m$	$10^{-10}m$	$10^{-12}m$

Our _eyes_ can only detect a _very narrow range_ of EM waves — the ones we call (visible) _light_.
All EM waves travel at _exactly_ the same _speed_ as light in a _vacuum_, and _pretty much_ the same speed as light in _other media_ like glass or water — though this is always _slower_ than their speed in vacuum.

When white light is shone through a prism then the colours disperse, due to these fractional changes in speed through the glass medium. You need to _learn this diagram_ and know that violet light _bends_ more than red (See P. 39).

As the Wavelength Changes, So Do the Properties

1) As the _wavelength_ of EM radiation changes, its _interaction_ with matter changes. In particular the way any EM wave is _absorbed_, _reflected_ or _transmitted_ by any given substance depends _entirely_ on its _wavelength_ — that's the whole point of these three pages of course!
2) As a rule the EM waves at _each end_ of the spectrum tend to be able to _pass through_ material, whilst those _nearer the middle_ are _absorbed_.
3) Also, the ones at the _top end_ (high frequency, short wavelength) tend to be the most _dangerous_, whilst those lower down are generally _harmless_.
4) When _any_ EM radiation is _absorbed_ it can cause _two effects_:
   a) _Heating_   b) Creation of a _tiny alternating current_ with the _same_ frequency as the radiation.
5) You need to know all the details that follow about all the different parts of the EM spectrum:

Radio Waves Are Used Mainly for Communications

1) _Radio Waves_ are used mainly for _communication_ and, perhaps more importantly, for controlling model aeroplanes.
2) Both _TV and FM Radio_ use _short wavelength_ radio waves of about _1m wavelength_.
3) To receive these wavelengths you need to be more or less in _direct sight_ of the transmitter, because they will _not_ bend (diffract) over hills or travel very far _through_ buildings.
4) The _longer wavelengths_ can travel further because they are _reflected_ from an _electrically charged layer_ in the Earth's upper atmosphere (the ionosphere). This means they can be sent further around the Earth.

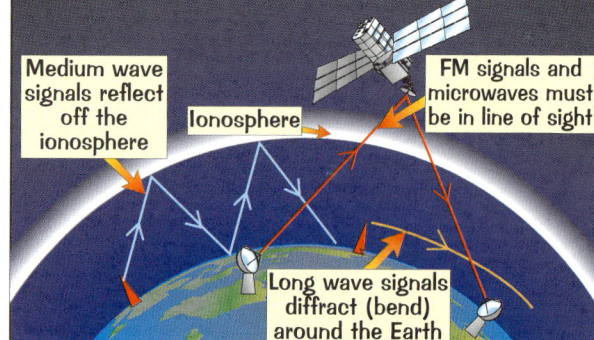

The spectrum — isn't that something kinda rude in Biology...

There are lots of details on this page that you definitely need to know. The top diagram is an absolute must — they usually give it to you with one or two missing labels to fill in. _Learn_ the three sections on this page, then _scribble_ a _mini-essay_ for each to see what you know.

SEG Syllabus   SECTION THREE — WAVES

Microwaves and Infrared

The Electromagnetic Spectrum

Microwaves Are Used for Cooking and Satellite Signals

1) _Microwaves_ have _two_ main uses: _cooking_ food and _satellite_ transmissions.
2) These two applications use two _different frequencies_ of microwaves.
3) Satellite transmissions use a frequency that _passes easily_ through the _Earth's atmosphere_ — including _clouds_. 
4) The frequency used for _cooking_, on the other hand, is one that's readily _absorbed_ by _water molecules_. This is how a microwave oven works. The microwaves pass easily _into the food_ and are then _absorbed_ by the _water molecules_, heating the food from the _inside_.
5) Microwaves can therefore be _dangerous_ because they can be absorbed by _living tissue_ and the heat will _damage or kill_ the cells, causing a sort of "_cold burn_".

Infrared Radiation — Night Vision and Remote Controls

1) _Infrared_ (or IR) is otherwise known as _heat radiation_. This is given out by all _hot objects_ and you _feel it_ on your _skin_ as _radiant heat_. Infrared is readily _absorbed_ by _all_ materials and _causes heating_.
2) _Radiant heaters_ (i.e. those that _glow red_, like _toasters_ and _grills_) use infrared radiation.
3) Infrared is also used for all the _remote controls_ of _TVs and videos_. It's ideal for sending _harmless_ signals over _short distances_ without _interfering_ with radio frequencies (like the TV channels).
4) Infrared is also used for _night-vision equipment_. The _police_ use this to spot miscreants _running away_, like you've seen on **TV**.

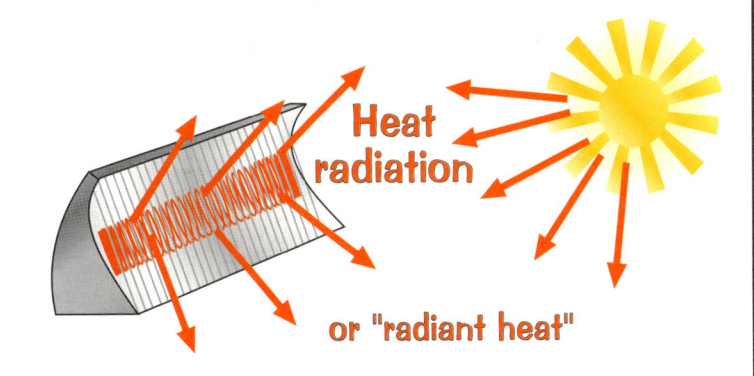

Microwaves — I thought you got those on calm beaches...

Each part of the EM spectrum is different, and you definitely need to know all the details about each type of radiation. These are just the kind of things they'll test in your Exams. Do _mini-essays_ for microwaves and IR. Then _check_ to see how you did. Then _try again... and again..._

SECTION THREE — WAVES

SEG SYLLABUS

Visible, UV, X-rays, γ-Rays

The Electromagnetic Spectrum

Visible light Is Used to See with and in Optical Fibres

Visible Light is pretty useful. We use it for seeing with for one thing. You could say (as indeed the syllabus does!) that a use of it is in an endoscope for seeing inside a patient's body, but let's face it — where do you draw the line? — it's also used in microscopes, telescopes, kaleidoscopes, pretend telescopes made of old toilet rolls, it's used for seeing in the dark (torch, lights, etc.) and for saying "hi" to people without speaking. Seriously though, it is also used in Optical Fibre Digital Communications, which is the best one by far for your answer in the Exam (see P. 40).

Ultraviolet Light Causes Skin Cancer

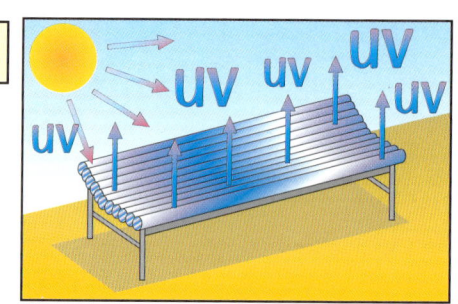

1) This is what causes sunburn and skin cancer if you spend too much time in the sun.
2) It also causes your skin to tan. Sunbeds give out UV rays, but less harmful ones than many of the Sun's.
3) Darker skin protects against UV rays by preventing them from reaching more vulnerable skin tissues deeper down.
4) There are special coatings that absorb UV light and then give out visible light instead. These are used to coat the insides of fluorescent tubes and lamps.
5) Ultraviolet is also useful for hidden security marks, which are written in special ink that can only be seen with an ultraviolet light.

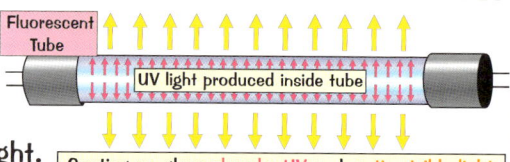

X-Rays Are Used in Hospitals, but Are Pretty Dangerous

1) These are used in hospitals to take X-ray photographs of people, e.g. to see if they have any broken bones.
2) X-rays pass easily through flesh, but not through denser materials like bone or metal.
3) X-rays can cause cancer, so radiographers, who take X-ray pictures all day long, wear lead aprons and stand behind a lead screen to keep their exposure to X-rays to a minimum.
4) X-rays can also be used in scientific research to examine the structure of crystals and other materials.

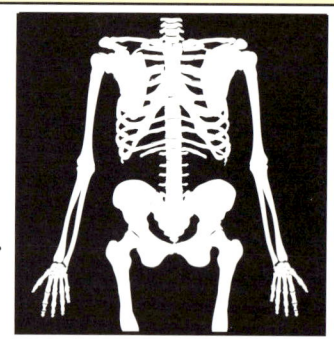

The brighter bits are where fewer X-rays get through. This is a negative image. The plate starts off all white.

Gamma Rays Cause Cancer, but Are Used to Treat It Too

1) Gamma rays are used to kill harmful bacteria in food to keep it fresher for longer.
2) They are also used to sterilise medical instruments, again by killing the bacteria.
3) They can also be used in the treatment of cancer because they kill cancer cells.
4) Gamma rays tend to pass through soft tissue, but some are absorbed by the cells.
5) In high doses, Gamma rays (along with X-rays and UV rays) can kill normal cells.
6) In lower doses all these three types of EM Waves can cause normal cells to become cancerous.

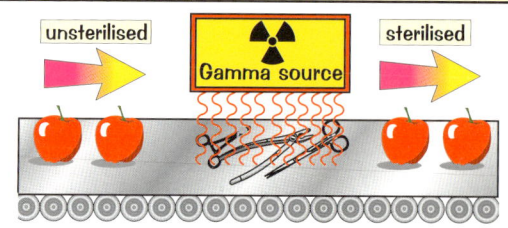

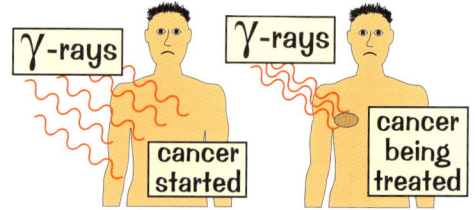

Radiographers are like teachers — they can see right through you...

Here are the other four parts of the EM spectrum for you to learn. Ace, isn't it. At least there's some groovy diagrams to help relieve the tedium. On this page there are four sections. Do a mini-essay for each section, then check, re-learn, re-scribble, re-check, etc. etc.

SEG Syllabus

SECTION THREE — WAVES

Sound Waves

1) Sound Travels as a Wave:

Sound can be _reflected_ off walls (echoes), and it can be _refracted_ as it passes into different media. These are standard properties of waves, so we deduce that _sound travels as a wave_. This "sound" reasoning can also be applied to deduce the wave nature of light.

2) Sound Waves Travel at Different Speeds in Different Media

1) _Sound Waves_ are caused by _vibrating_ objects.
2) Sound waves are _longitudinal_ waves that travel at _fixed speeds_ in particular _media_, as shown in the table.
3) As you can see, the _denser_ the medium, the _faster_ sound travels through it, generally speaking anyway.
4) Sound generally travels _faster in solids_ than in liquids, and faster in liquids than in gases.

Substance	Density	Speed of Sound
Iron	7.9 g/cm^3	5000 m/s
Rubber	0.9 g/cm^3	1600 m/s
Water	1.0 g/cm^3	1400 m/s
Cork	0.3 g/cm^3	500 m/s
Air	0.001 g/cm^3	330 m/s

3) Sound Doesn't Travel Through a Vacuum

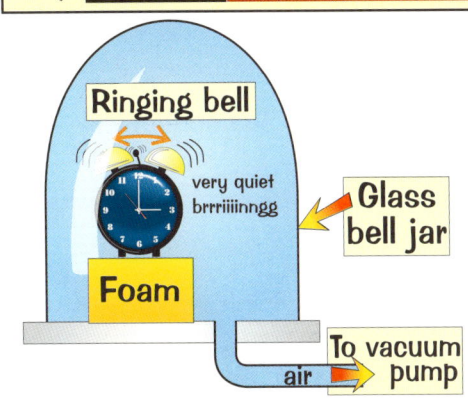

1) Sound waves can be _reflected_, _refracted_ and _diffracted_.
2) But one thing they _can't do_ is travel through a _vacuum_.
3) This is nicely demonstrated by the jolly old _bell jar experiment_.
4) As the air is _sucked out_ by the _vacuum pump_, the sound gets _quieter and quieter_.
5) The bell has to be _mounted_ on something like _foam_ to stop the sound from it travelling through the solid surface and making the bench vibrate, because you'd hear that instead.

4) Echoes and Reverberation Are Due to REFLECTED Sound

1) Sound will only be _reflected_ from _hard flat surfaces_. Things like _carpets_ and _curtains_ act as _absorbing surfaces_, which will _absorb_ sounds rather than reflect them.
2) This is very noticeable in the _reverberation_ of an _empty room_. A big empty room sounds _completely different_ once you've added carpet and curtains and a bit of furniture, because these things absorb the sound quickly and stop it _echoing_ (reverberating) around the room.

5) Amplitude Is a Measure of the Energy Carried by a Wave

1) The greater the AMPLITUDE, the _more_ ENERGY the wave carries.
2) With SOUND this means it'll be LOUDER.
3) _Bigger amplitude_ means a _louder sound_.
4) With LIGHT, a bigger amplitude means it'll be BRIGHTER.

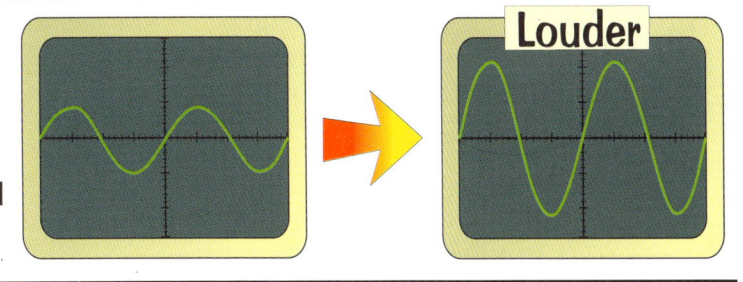

If sound travelled through vacuum — sunny days would be deafening...

Once again the page is broken up into five sections with numbered points for each. All those numbered points are important. They're all mentioned specifically in the syllabus so you should expect them to test exactly this stuff in the Exams. _Learn and enjoy_.

SECTION THREE — WAVES
SEG Syllabus

Sound Waves

Sound

The Frequency of a Sound Wave Determines Its Pitch

1) High frequency sound waves sound HIGH PITCHED like a squeaking mouse.
2) Low frequency sound waves sound LOW PITCHED like a mooing cow.
3) Frequency is the number of complete vibrations each second. It's measured in hertz (Hz).
4) Other common units are kHz (1,000 Hz) and MHz (1,000,000 Hz).
5) High frequency (or high pitch) also means shorter wavelength.
6) The range of frequencies heard by humans is from about 20Hz to 20kHz.
7) These CRO screens are very important, so make sure you know all about them:

Original Sound

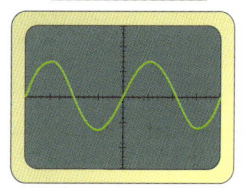

The CRO screens tell us about the pitch and loudness of the sound:

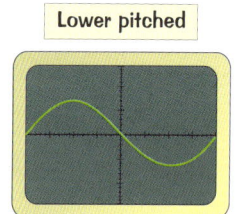

Lower pitched

2) When the peaks are further apart then the sound is at a lower pitch (a lower frequency).

Higher pitched

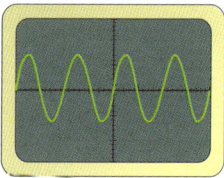

1) The closer the peaks are together, the higher pitched the sound (and the higher the frequency).

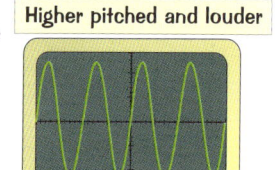

Higher pitched and louder

3) The CRO screen will show large peaks for a loud noise (sound waves with a big amplitude).

Microphones Turn Sound Waves into Electrical Signals

1) An electrical "signal" is simply a varying electrical current.
2) The variations in the current carry the information.
3) The currents from a microphone are very small and are amplified into much bigger signals by an amplifier.
4) These signals from the microphone can be recorded and played back through speakers.

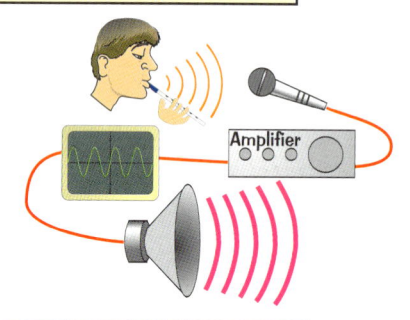

Loudspeakers Turn Electrical Signals into Sound Waves

1) AC electrical signals from the amplifier are fed to the speaker coil.
2) This produces a magnetic field when the current changes, which attracts or repels the magnet in the speaker, moving the cone of the speaker back or forth.
3) This motion generates sound waves.
4) So speakers turn electrical signals into sound waves — exactly the opposite of a microphone.

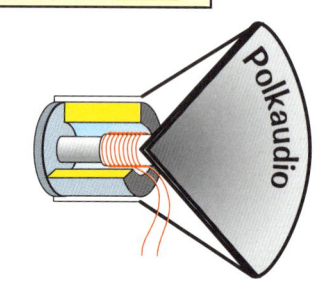

Pitch — doesn't that have something to do with football...

Just three sections here, but its important stuff. And the simple truth is that you've just gotta know it if you want those Exam marks. You do realise I hope that most Exam questions, even in Physics, simply test whether or not you've learned the basic facts. Just easy marks really.

SEG Syllabus

SECTION THREE — WAVE

Ultrasound

Sound

Ultrasound Is Sound with a Higher Frequency Than We Can Hear

Devices can be made that produce _electrical oscillations_ at virtually _any frequency_. These can easily be converted into _mechanical vibrations_ to produce _sound_ waves _beyond the range_ of _human hearing_ (i.e. frequencies above 20kHz). This is called ULTRASOUND, and it has loads of uses:

Detecting with Ultrasound

1) The ultrasound waves are _transmitted_ through a _metal casting_ and whenever they reach the boundary between two _media_ (like metal and air), some of the wave is _reflected back_ and detected at the surface. The wave will reflect from the cracks in the casting because of the change in medium from metal to air.
2) The rest of the wave _continues_ through the casting and _more of the wave_ is reflected back (as echoes) at each _boundary_.
3) The exact _timing and distribution_ of these _echoes_ give detailed _information_ about the internal _structure_ of the casting.
4) The details are then _processed_ by _computer_ to produce a _visual display_ of the casting.

Two other uses for ultrasound:

1) Foetal Imaging

In pre-natal scanning the skin will normally reflect most of the ultrasound, so _saline gel_ is applied to the skin to improve the _transmission_ of the ultrasound.

The sound waves will pass through the skin and _reflect_ from the _surface of the foetus_.

These reflected waves are _detected_ at the _probe_ and converted into a _visual display_.

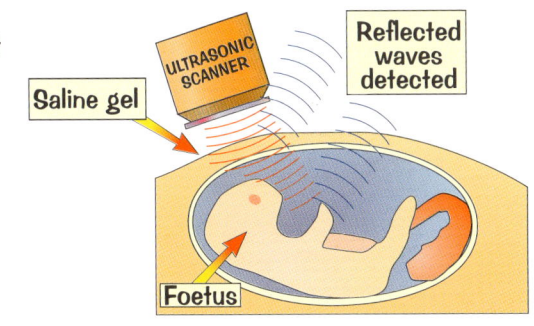

2) Range and Direction Finding — SONAR

Bats send out _high-pitched squeaks_ (ultrasound) and pick up the _reflections_ with their _big ears_. Their brains are able to _process_ the reflected signal and turn it into a _picture_ of what's around.
So the bats basically "_see_" with _sound waves_, well enough in fact to catch _moths_ in _mid-flight_ in complete _darkness_ — it's a nice trick if you can do it.

The same technique is used for _SONAR_, which uses _sound waves underwater_ to detect features on the sea-bed. The _pattern_ of the reflections indicates the _depth_ and basic features.

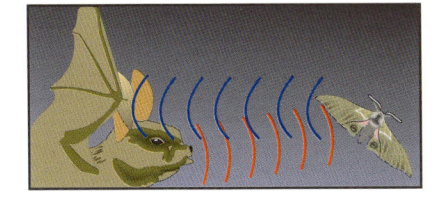

Ultrasound — weren't they a pop group...

Geesh — you wouldn't think there was much more to say on sound by now. But ultrasound often appears in those lovely Exams, so I'd suggest you learn it. Start with the headings, then learn the points below each, _cover the page_, and _scribble a mini-essay_ for each, with diagrams.

SECTION THREE — WAVES

SEG SYLLABUS

The Speed of Sound

Relative Speeds of Sound and Light

1) *Light* travels about *a million times faster* than *sound*, so you never bother to calculate how long it takes compared to sound. You only work out the time taken for the *sound* to travel.
2) The *formula* needed is always the good old $s{=}d/t$ one for *speed, distance and time* (see P. 21).
3) When you see something making a sound more than about *100m away*, the effect is quite *noticeable*. Good examples are:
a) *LIVE CRICKET* — you hear the *"knock"* a while after seeing the ball being struck.
b) *HAMMERING* — you hear the *"clang"* when the hammer is back up *in mid air*.
c) *STARTING PISTOL* — you *see the smoke* and then *hear the bang*.
d) *JET AIRCRAFT* — they're always *ahead* of where the sound's coming from.
e) *THUNDER AND LIGHTNING* — the flash of lightning causes the sound of the thunder, and the *time interval* between the *flash* and the *rumble* tells you how far away the lightning is. There's approximately a *five second delay for every mile*. (1 mile = 1,600m, ÷ 330 = 4.8s)

EXAMPLE: Looking out from his modest office across the Designated (EU Directive 672) Young Persons Recreation Area (i.e. the school yard), the Headmaster saw the five most troublesome and nauseating kids in his school destroying something nice with their horrid hammer. Before acting swiftly, he did take the time to notice that there was a delay of exactly 0.4 seconds between the hammer striking and the sound reaching his shell-like ear. So just how far away were these horrid children? (Sound travels at 330m/s in air, as you know).

ANSWER: The formula we want is of course "Speed = Distance/Time" or "s=d/t". We want to find the distance, d. We already know the time is 0.4s, and the speed of sound in air = 330m/s. Hence d=s×t (from the triangle). This gives: d = 330×0.4 = *132m*. (That's how far the sound travels in 0.4 secs). Easy peasy.

Echo Questions — Don't Forget the Factor of Two

1) The *big thing* to remember with *echo questions* is that because the sound has to travel *both ways*, then to get the *right answer* you'll need to either *double something* or *halve something*.
2) Make sure you remember: sound travels at about *330m/s in air* and *1,400m/s in water*. Any echo question will likely be in air or water and if you have to work out the speed of the sound it's real useful to know what sort of number you should be getting. So for example, if you get 170m/s for the speed of sound in air then you should realise you've *forgotten the factor of two* somewhere, and then you can *easily go back and sort it*.

EXAMPLE: Having successfully expelled the five most troublesome and nauseating kids from his school, the jubilant Headmaster popped open a bottle of Champagne and heard the echo 0.6s later from the other side of his modest office. Just how big was this modest office?

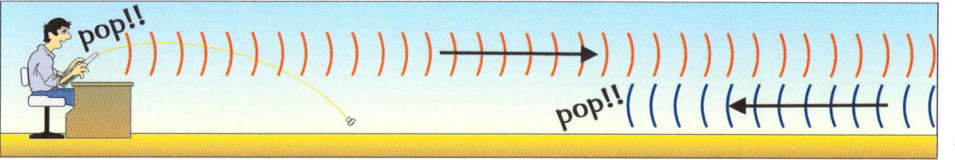

ANSWER: The formula is of course "Speed = Distance/Time" or "s=d/t". We want to find the distance, d. We already know the time, 0.6s, and the speed (of sound in air), hence d=s×t (from the triangle). This gives: d = 330×0.6 = 198m. But Watch out! *Don't forget the factor of two for echo questions:* The 0.6 secs is for *there and back*, so the office is only *half* that distance — *99m long*.

Learn about echoes and the factor of two...factor of two...factor of two...

Learn the details on this page, then *cover it up* and *scribble them down*. Then try these:
1) A man sees the cricketer hit the ball and hears the knock 0.6s later. How far away is he?
2) A ship sends a sonar signal to the sea bed and detects the echo 0.7s later. How deep is it?

Seismic Waves

Sound

Seismic Waves Reveal the Earth's Structure

1) <u>Seismic waves</u> are caused by <u>earthquakes</u>. They're pretty handy for telling us what the Earth's like inside. Without them, we'd only know about the first <u>10km</u> or so — that's how far we can <u>drill</u>.
2) Measurements of the waves reveal that the Earth has a <u>core</u>, which is divided into an <u>inner core</u> (pretty <u>solid</u>) and an <u>outer core</u> (<u>liquid</u>).
3) Outside the core you've got the <u>mantle</u>, which is basically <u>pretty solid</u>, though it does <u>flow a bit</u> under the enormous <u>pressures</u>.
4) The final bit is the <u>crust</u>, which ranges in thickness from about 10km under the oceans to about 80km under the highest mountains. Pretty <u>flimsy</u> really — that's all there is between us and the <u>fiery depths</u>.

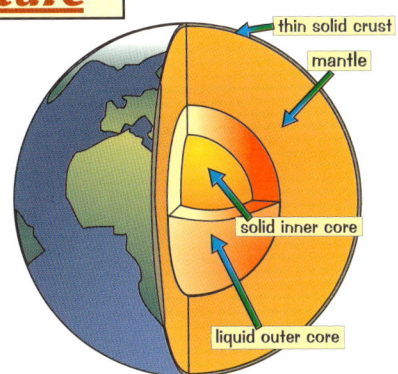

thin solid crust
mantle
solid inner core
liquid outer core

S-Waves and P-Waves Take Different Paths

P-Waves Are Longitudinal

<u>P-Waves</u> travel through both <u>solids and liquids</u>. They travel <u>faster</u> than <u>S-waves</u>.

No P-waves reach here

P-waves pass through core and are detected here

S-Waves Are TranSverSe

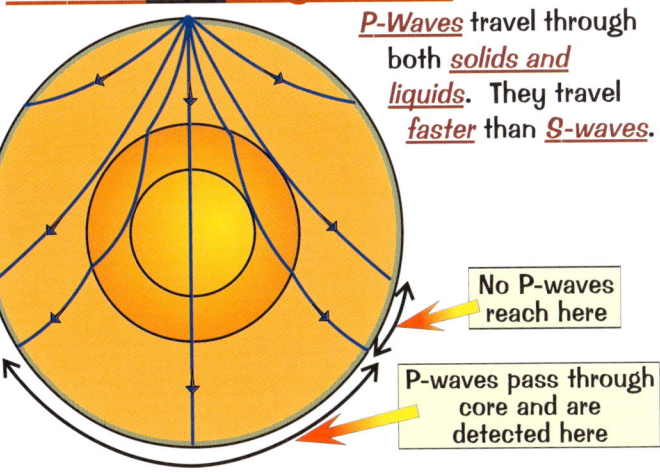

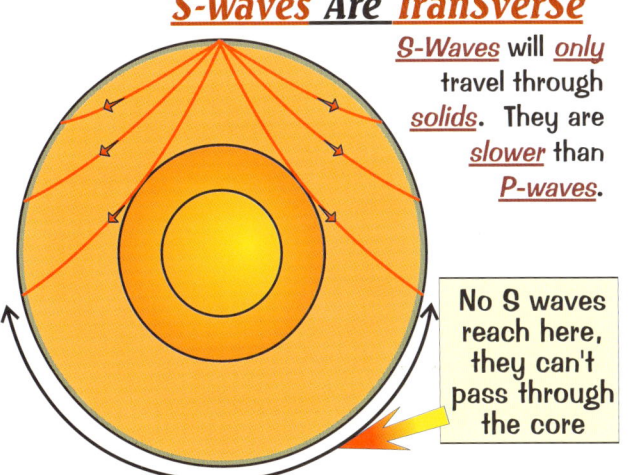

<u>S-Waves</u> will <u>only</u> travel through <u>solids</u>. They are <u>slower</u> than <u>P-waves</u>.

No S waves reach here, they can't pass through the core

Seismographs Tells Us What's Down There

1) About <u>halfway</u> through the Earth, there's an abrupt <u>change in direction</u> of both types of wave. This indicates that there's a sudden <u>increase in density</u> at that point — the <u>CORE</u>.
2) The fact that S-waves are <u>not</u> detected in the <u>shadow</u> of this core tells us that it's very <u>liquid</u>.
3) It's also found that <u>P-waves</u> travel <u>slightly faster</u> through the <u>middle</u> of the core, which strongly suggests that there's a <u>solid inner core</u>.
4) Note that <u>S-waves</u> do travel through the <u>mantle</u>, which suggests that it's kinda <u>solid</u>, though I always thought it was made of <u>molten lava</u> which looks pretty <u>liquidy</u> to me when it comes <u>sploshing</u> out of volcanoes. Still there you go, just another one of life's little conundrums, I guess.

The Paths Curve Due to Increasing Density (Causing Refraction)

1) Both <u>S-waves</u> and <u>P-waves</u> travel <u>faster</u> in <u>more dense</u> material.
2) The <u>curvature</u> of their paths is due to the <u>increasing density</u> of the <u>mantle</u> and <u>core</u> with depth.
3) When the density changes <u>suddenly</u>, the waves change direction <u>abruptly</u>, as shown above.
4) The paths <u>curve</u> because the density of both the mantle and the core <u>increases steadily</u> with increasing depth. The waves <u>gradually change direction</u> because their speed is <u>gradually changing</u>, due to gradual changes in the <u>density</u> of the medium. This is <u>refraction</u>, of course.

Seismic waves — they reveal the terrible trembling truth...

The last page on waves. Hoorah. Once again there are four main sections to learn. <u>Learn</u> the headings first, then try <u>scribbling down</u> all the details for each heading, including the diagrams. Remember that S-waves are tran**S**ver**S**e — so P-waves must be the longitudinal ones.

SECTION THREE — WAVES

SEG SYLLABUS

Revision Summary for Section Three

One thing's for sure — there are loads of fairly easy facts to learn about waves. Of course there are still some bits that need thinking about, but really, most of it is fairly easy stuff that just needs learning. Don't forget, this book contains all the important information that they've specifically mentioned in the syllabus, and this is precisely the stuff they're going to test you on in the Exams. You must practise these questions over and over again until they're easy.

1) Sketch a wave and mark on it the amplitude and wavelength.
2) Sketch a transverse wave. Give a definition for it. Give four examples of transverse waves.
3) Sketch a longitudinal wave. Give a definition for it. Give two examples of longitudinal waves.
4) Define frequency, amplitude and wavelength for a wave.
5) Give three examples of waves carrying energy.
6) What are the two formulas involved with waves? How do you decide which one to use?
7) What are the standard units for: a) wavelength b) frequency c) velocity d) time?
8) Convert these to standard units: a) 500kHz b) 35cm c) 4.6MHz d) 4cm/s e) 2½ mins
9) Find the speed of a wave with frequency 50kHz and wavelength 0.3cm.
10) Find the frequency of a wave of wavelength 1.5km and speed 3×10^8 m/s.
11) Sketch the patterns when plane ripples reflect at a) a plane surface, b) a curved surface.
12) Sketch the reflection of curved ripples at a plane surface.
13) What is the law of reflection? Are sound and light reflected?
14) Draw a neat ray diagram to show how to locate the position of the image in a plane mirror.
15) What is refraction? What causes it? How does it affect wavelength and frequency?
16) Sketch a ray of light going through a rectangular glass block, showing the angles i and r.
17) How fast does light go in glass? Which way does it bend as it enters glass? What if i=90°?
18) What is dispersion? Sketch a diagram to show it, with all the labels.
19) Sketch the three diagrams to illustrate Total Internal Reflection and the Critical Angle.
20) Sketch two applications of total internal reflection that use 45° prisms, and explain them.
21) Give details of the two main uses of optical fibres. How do optical fibres work?
22) What is diffraction? Sketch the diffraction of a) water waves b) sound waves c) light.
23) What aspect of EM waves determines their differing properties?
24) Sketch the EM spectrum with all its details. What happens when EM waves are absorbed?
25) Give full details of the uses of radio waves.
26) Give full details of the two main uses of microwaves, and the three main uses of infrared.
27) Give a sensible example of the use of visible light. What is its main use?
28) Detail three uses of UV light, two uses of X-rays and three uses of gamma rays.
29) What harm will UV, X-rays and gamma rays do in *high* doses? What about in *low* doses?
30) Write down some typical speeds for sound in different materials.
31) Describe the bell jar experiment. What does it demonstrate?
32) What's an echo? What is reverberation? What affects reverberation in a room?
33) What's the connection between amplitude and the energy carried by a wave?
34) What effect does greater amplitude have on a) sound waves b) light waves?
35) What's the relationship between frequency and pitch for a sound wave?
36) Sketch CRO screens showing high and low pitch, and quiet and loud sounds.
37) What is ultrasound? Give details of two applications of ultrasound.
38) How do the speeds of sound and light compare? Give five examples that show the difference.
39) A crash of thunder is heard 6 seconds after the flash of lightning. How far away is it?
40) If the sea bed is 600m down, how long will it take to receive a sonar echo from it?
41) What causes seismic waves? Sketch diagrams showing the paths of both types, and explain.
42) What do seismographs tell us about the structure of the Earth? Describe the Earth's inner structure.

SEG Syllabus

SECTION THREE — WAVES

THE EARTH & BEYOND

The Solar System

The _order_ of the planets can be remembered with this little jollyism:

Mercury, Venus, Earth, Mars, Jupiter, Saturn, Uranus, Neptune, Pluto
(My Very Energetic Mum Just Swam Under North Pier)

MERCURY, VENUS, EARTH and MARS are known as the INNER PLANETS.
JUPITER, SATURN, URANUS, NEPTUNE and PLUTO are much further away and are the OUTER PLANETS.

The Planets Don't Give Out Light, They Just Reflect the Sun's

1) You can _see_ some of the nearer planets with the _naked eye_ at night, e.g. Mars and Venus.
2) They look just like _stars_, but they are of course _totally different_.
3) Stars are _huge_ and _very far away_ and _give out_ lots of light.
   The planets are _smaller and nearer_ and they just _reflect the sunlight_ falling on them.
4) Planets always _orbit around stars_. In our Solar System the planets orbit the _Sun_ of course.
5) All the planets in our Solar System orbit in the _same plane_, except Pluto (as shown).
6) The orbits of the planets are _slightly elliptical_ (elongated circles).

The Sun Is a Star, Giving Out All Types of EM Radiation

1) The Sun, like other stars, produces _heat_ from _nuclear fusion reactions_ that turn _hydrogen into helium_. This makes it really hot.
2) It gives out the _full spectrum_ of _electromagnetic radiation_.

The Relative Sizes of the Planets and the Sun

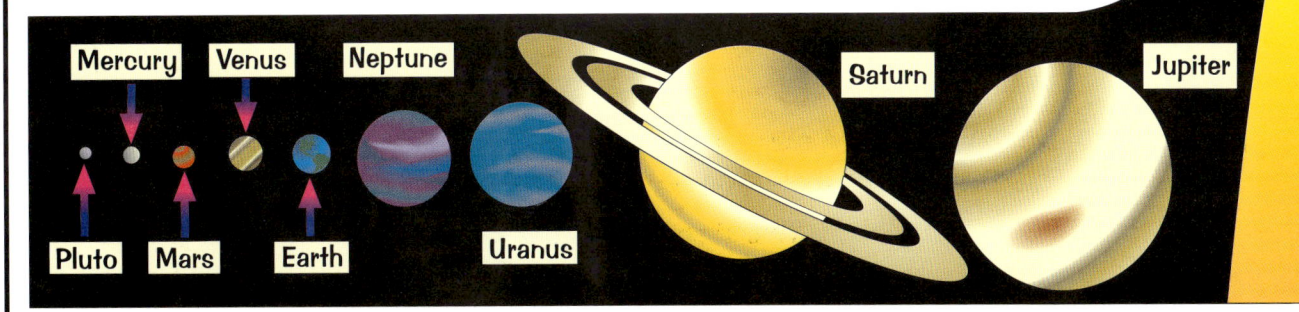

Learn the planets — they can be quite illuminating...

Isn't the Solar System great! All those pretty coloured planets and all that big black empty space. You can look forward to one or two easy questions on the planets — or you might get two real horrors instead. Be ready: _learn_ all the _nitty gritty details_ till you know it all real good.

SECTION FOUR — THE EARTH & BEYOND   SEG SYLLABUS

The Planets

The Solar System

Gravity Is the Force That Keeps Everything in Orbit

1) *Gravity* is a force of *attraction* that acts between *all* masses.
2) With *very large* masses like *stars* and *planets*, the force is *very big* and acts *a long way out*.
3) So the *closer* a planet gets to the Sun, the *stronger* the *force of attraction*. 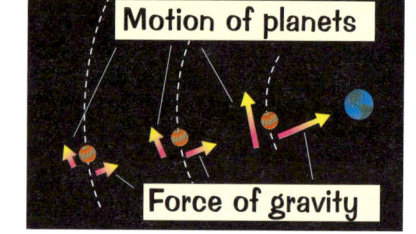
4) To *counteract* this stronger gravity, the planet must move *faster* and cover its orbit *quicker*.
5) *Comets* are also held in *orbit* by gravity, as are *moons* and *satellites* and *space stations*.

The Inverse Square Law

The size of the force of gravity follows the fairly famous *"inverse square"* relationship. The main effect of that is that the force *decreases very quickly* with increasing *distance*. The *formula* is $F \propto 1/d^2$, but I reckon it's *easier* just to remember the basic idea *in words*:

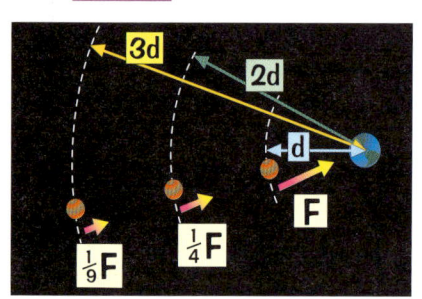

a) If you **DOUBLE the distance** from a planet, the size of the *force* will *decrease* by a *factor of FOUR* (2^2).
b) If you **TREBLE the distance**, the *force* of gravity will *decrease* by a *factor of NINE* (3^2), and so on.
c) On the other hand, if you get **TWICE as close** the gravity becomes **FOUR times stronger**.

Higher Higher

Planets in the Night Sky Seem to Move Across the Constellations

1) The stars in the sky form *fixed patterns* called *constellations*.
2) These all stay *fixed* in *relation to each other* and simply *"rotate"* as the Earth spins.
3) The *planets* look *just like stars*, except that they *wander* across the constellations over periods of *days or weeks* — or even *years* for the really *way-out* ones like Pluto.
4) Their position and movement depends on where they are *in their orbit*, compared to us.
5) Many early astronomers thought that the Earth remained stationary, and all the stars and planets rotated around it. However the *peculiar movement* of the planets made astronomers like Copernicus realise that the Earth *wasn't the centre of the Universe* after all, but was in fact just *the third rock from the Sun*. It's *very strong evidence* for the *Sun-centred* model of the Solar System.
6) Alas, the boys at the *Spanish Inquisition* were less than keen on such heresy, and poor old *Copernicus* had a pretty hard time of it for a while. In the end though, *"the truth will out"*.

There's been many other theories about the Earth's structure and the organisation of the Solar System. Their acceptance or rejection often depended as much on their social and historical context (like what the Church thought at that time) than on science.

Learn this page — but keep shtum to the boys in the red robes...

Planets are ace aren't they. And it's all down to gravity. The best bit is you can usually see one or two of them in the night sky, just by lifting your eyes to the heavens. *Learn* all the little bits on this page, then *cover and scribble*. And keep going till you know it all. *Enjoy*.

SEG Syllabus SECTION FOUR — THE EARTH & BEYOND

Moons, Asteroids and Comets

The Solar System

Moons Are Sometimes Called Natural Satellites

The planets in our solar system are all natural satellites of the Sun. The planets also have their own natural satellites (moons):

1) The Earth only has one moon of course, but some of the other planets have quite a few.

2) We can only see the Moon because it reflects sunlight.

3) The phases of the Moon happen depending on where the moon is in its orbit. The position of the Moon determines how much of its illuminated side we can see.

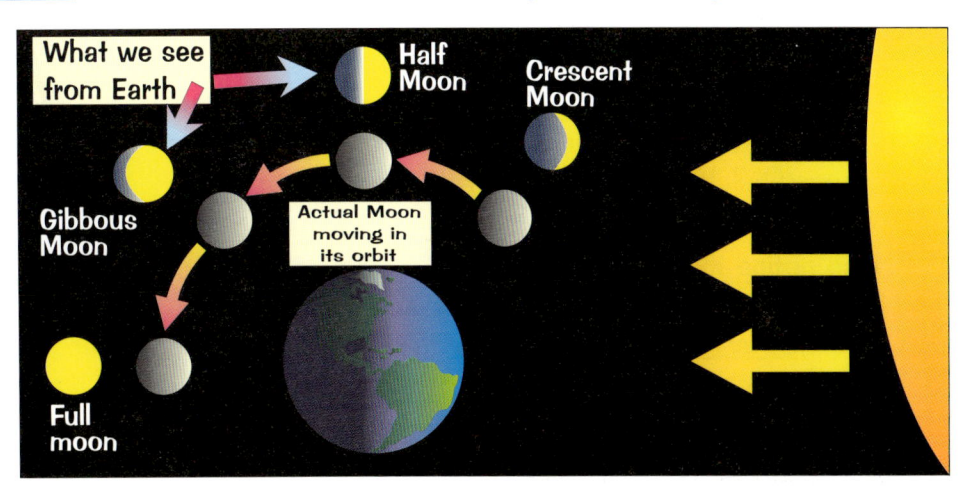

Asteroids are Rocks Orbiting in a Belt Between Mars and Jupiter

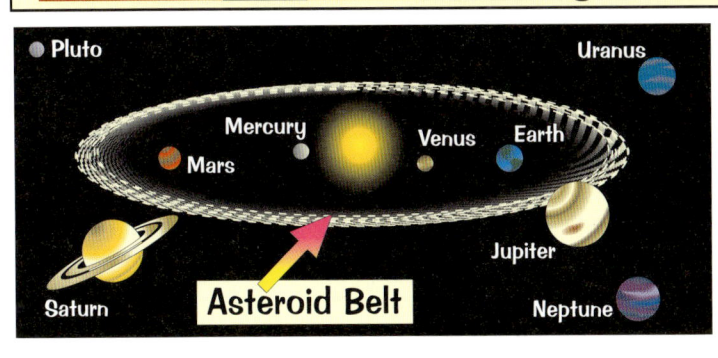

1) There are several thousand lumps of rock orbiting the Sun in a belt between the orbits of Mars and Jupiter.
2) They vary in size from about 1,000 km diameter down to less than 1 km.
3) These asteroids usually stay in their orbits, but if they collide and get knocked out of their orbits, they could become meteorites...

Comets Orbit the Sun, but Have Very Eccentric (Elongated) Orbits

1) Comets only appear once in a while because their orbits take them very far from the Sun and then back in close, which is when we see them. This can take anything from a few years to several thousand years.
2) The Sun is not at the centre of the orbit but near to one end, as shown.
3) Comet orbits can be in different planes from the orbits of the planets.
4) Comets are made of ice and rock. As they approach the Sun the ice melts, leaving a bright tail of debris which can be millions of km long.
5) The comet travels much faster when it's nearer the Sun than when it's in the more distant part of its orbit. This is because the pull of gravity makes it speed up as it gets closer, and then slows it down as it gets further away from the Sun.

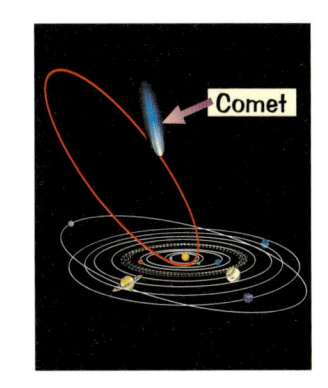

Learn about these lumps of rock — and watch out for them...

Three more cosmic bits and bobs for you to know about. There's more to the Solar System than just planets you know. Make sure you learn all the details about these different lumps of rock. It's all in the syllabus, so they could ask you about any of it. Mini-essays please. Now.

SECTION FOUR — THE EARTH & BEYOND

SEG SYLLABUS

The Cause of Days and Seasons

The Solar System

The Rotation of the Earth Causes Day and Night

1) As the Earth slowly rotates any point on the Earth's surface moves from the bright side in the sunlight round into the darkness. As the Earth keeps rotating it eventually comes back into the sunshine again.
   This sequence describes day-dusk-night-dawn.

2) A full rotation takes 24 hours of course — a full day. Next time you watch the Sun set, try to imagine yourself helpless on that big rotating ball as you move silently across the twilight zone and into the shadows.

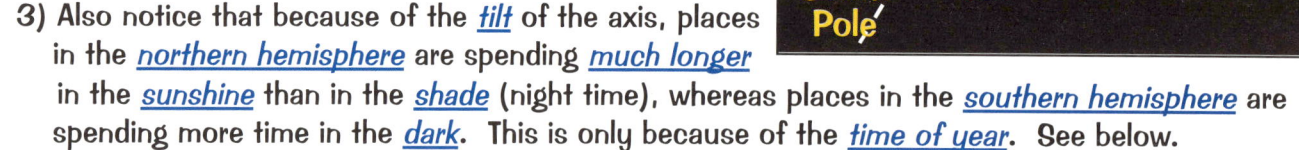

3) Also notice that because of the tilt of the axis, places in the northern hemisphere are spending much longer in the sunshine than in the shade (night time), whereas places in the southern hemisphere are spending more time in the dark. This is only because of the time of year. See below.

4) Also notice that the further towards the poles you get, the longer the days are in summer and the longer the nights are in winter. Places *inside* the arctic circle have 24 hours a day of sunlight in midsummer, whilst in midwinter the Sun never rises at all.

5) At the equator, by contrast, the length of day never varies from one season to the next. It's always 12 hours of day and 12 hours of night. The position of the shadows shows all this.

The Orbit of the Earth Around the Sun Takes 365¼ Days

One full orbit of the Earth around the Sun is approximately 365 days (one year). This is split up into the seasons:

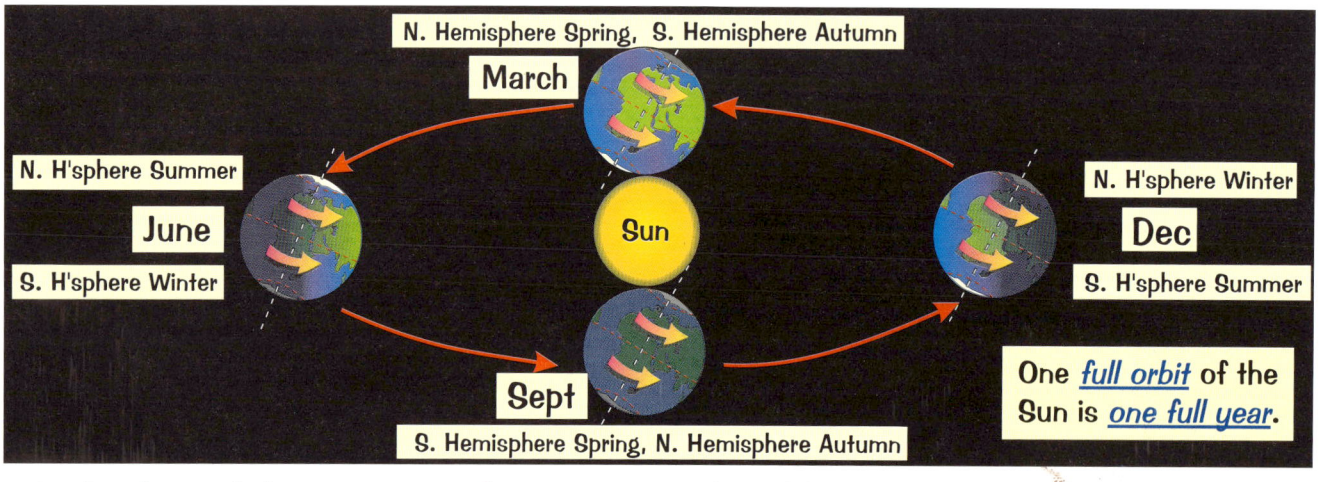

One full orbit of the Sun is one full year.

In the dim and distant past early astronomers thought that the Sun and all the planets orbited the Earth. i.e. that the Earth was the centre of the Universe.
   As we all know this was very wrong, but then they also thought the Earth was flat, and that the moon was made of cheese.

See Norway at Christmas — take a good torch...

This stuff about what causes the Sun to seem to "rise" and "set" and how the seasons are caused is surely irresistible-just-gotta-know-all-about-it kind of information, isn't it? Surely you must be filled with burning curiosity about it every time the dawn breaks — aren't you?

Satellites

The Solar System

Artificial Satellites Are Very Useful

They're called "*artificial*" satellites because moons are sometimes called "*natural*" satellites.

Low Polar Orbit Satellites Are for Weather and Spying

1) In a *low polar orbit* the satellite sweeps over *both poles* whilst the Earth *rotates beneath it*.
2) The time taken for each full orbit is just *a few hours*.
3) Each time the satellite comes round it can *scan* the next bit of the globe.
4) This allows the *whole surface* of the planet to be *monitored* each day.
5) These satellites are used for *monitoring the weather* and for *observing the Earth* (which could mean *spying*, or it could mean looking at things like *forests* or *rock deposits*).

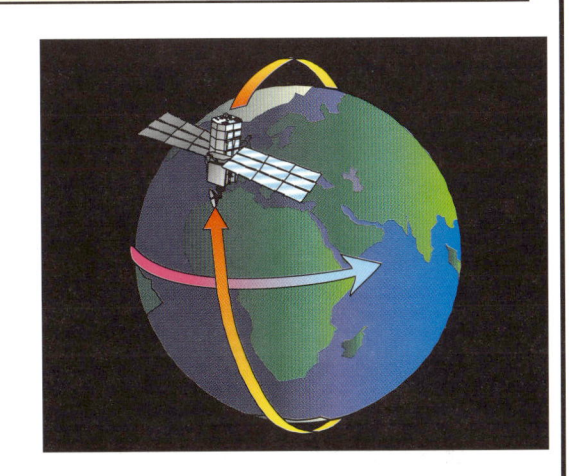

The Hubble Telescope Has No Atmosphere in the Way

1) The *big advantage* of having telescopes on *satellites* is that they can look out into space *without* the *distortion* and *blurring* caused by the Earth's *atmosphere*.
2) This allows *much greater detail* to be seen of *distant stars* and also the *planets* in the Solar System.

Satellites have also been put in orbits around other planets in the Solar System like Venus and Mars — for an even better view of these planets' surfaces.

Geostationary Satellites Are Used for Communications

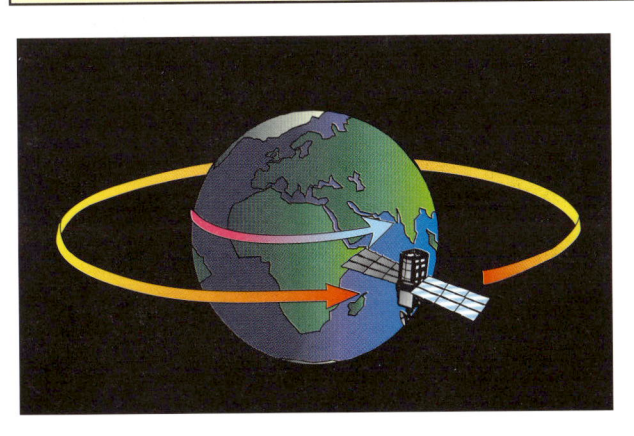

1) These are also called *geosynchronous satellites*.
2) They are put in quite a *high orbit* over the *equator* that takes *exactly 24 hours* to complete.
3) This means that they stay *above the same point* on the Earth's surface because the Earth *rotates with them* — hence the name geo(-Earth) stationary.
4) This makes them *ideal* for *telephone and TV* because they're always in the *same place* and they can *transfer signals* from one side of the Earth to the other in a *fraction of a second*.

Learn about satellites — and look down on your friends...

You can actually see the low polar orbit satellites on a nice dark clear night. They look like stars except they move quite fast in a dead straight line across the sky. You're never gonna spot the geostationary ones though. *Learn all the details* about satellites, ready for seizing juicy marks.

SECTION FOUR — THE EARTH & BEYOND

SEG SYLLABUS

The Universe

Our Sun Is in the Milky Way Galaxy

1) The Sun is one of many billions of stars that form the Milky Way galaxy.
2) The distances between neighbouring stars are usually millions of times greater than the distances between the planets in our Solar System. The Milky Way is 100,000 light years across.
3) The nearest star to us (apart from the Sun of course) is 4.2 light years away.
4) Gravity is of course the force that keeps the stars together in a galaxy and, like most things in the Universe, the galaxies all rotate, kinda like a catherine wheel, only much slower.
5) Our Sun is out in one of the spiral arms of the Milky Way galaxy.

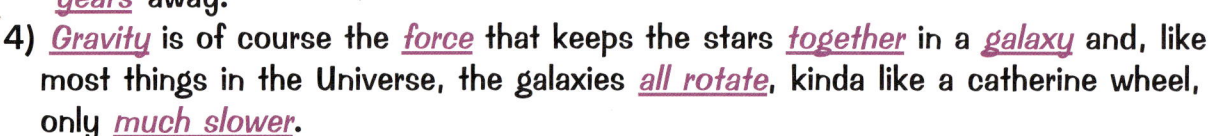

The Whole Universe Has More Than a Billion Galaxies

1) Galaxies themselves are often millions of times further apart than the stars are within a galaxy. That's millions of light years.
2) So you'll soon begin to realise that the Universe is mostly empty space and is really really big. Ever been to the NEC? Yeah? Well, it's even bigger than that.

A "Light Year" Is NOT a Period of Time — It's a Distance

Try and remember this will you. A light year is just a big distance through space:

A LIGHT YEAR is the DISTANCE that light travels IN ONE YEAR

2) To get this in km you first multiply the speed of light by the number of seconds in a year:
So one light year = 300,000,000 m/s × (60×60×24×365¼) secs = 9.5×10^{15} m
So 4.2 light years will be 4.2 × (9.5×10^{15}) = 4×10^{16} m or 40,000,000,000,000 km.
(Hmm, best take a few butties, eh?)

Galaxies, the Milky Way — it's just like a big chocolate factory...

More gripping facts about the Universe. It's just so big — look at those numbers: 1 light year is 9½ million million km, our galaxy is 100,000 of those across, and the Universe contains billions of galaxies, many of them separated by millions of light years. Man, that's what I call big.

The Origin of the Universe

Evolution of the Universe & Stars

The _Big Bang theory_ is our most _convincing_ theory of the origin of the Universe — though it's not the only one.

Red-Shift Needs Explaining

There are _TWO important bits of evidence_ you need to know about:

1) Light from Other Galaxies Is Red-Shifted

1) When we look at _light_ from distant _galaxies_ we find that _all the frequencies_ are _shifted_ towards the _red end_ of the spectrum.
2) In other words the _frequencies_ are all _slightly lower_ than they should be. This is because the galaxies are all _moving away from us_. It's the same effect as a car _horn_ sounding lower-pitched when the car is travelling _away_ from you. The sound _drops in frequency_.
3) This is called the _Doppler effect_.
4) _Measurements_ of the red-shift suggest that _all_ the distant galaxies are _moving away from us_ very quickly — and it's the _same_ whatever direction you look in.

2) The Further Away a Galaxy Is, the Greater the Red-Shift

1) _More distant galaxies_ have _greater_ red-shifts than nearer ones.
2) This means that more distant galaxies are _moving away faster_ than nearer ones.
3) The _inescapable conclusion_ appears to be that the whole Universe is _expanding_.

The Big Bang Theory — How It All Started

1) Since all the galaxies appear to be _moving apart_ very rapidly, the obvious _conclusion_ is that there was an _initial explosion_: the _Big Bang_.
2) All the matter in the Universe must have been _compressed_ into a _very small space_, which then rapidly expanded. The _expansion_ is still going on today.
3) The Big Bang is believed to have happened around _15 billion years ago_.
4) The age of the Universe can be _estimated_ from the current rate of _expansion_.
5) These estimates are _not very accurate_ because it's hard to tell how much the expansion has _slowed down_ since the Big Bang.
6) The rate at which the expansion is _slowing down_ is an _important factor_ in deciding the _future_ of the Universe.
7) _Without gravity_ the Universe would expand at the _same rate forever_.
8) However, the _attraction_ between all the mass in the Universe tends to _slow_ the expansion down.

Red shift — it's all in black and white before you...

The thing to learn here is the importance of _red shift_. It's what tells us that the Universe must have had a beginning. So _learn_ all those little points, then _cover them up_ and _jot them down_, then on your lunch-break you can ponder the mysteries of the universe over those sarnies.

SECTION FOUR — THE EARTH & BEYOND

The Life Cycle of Stars

Evolution of the Universe & Stars

Stars go through <u>many traumatic stages</u> in their lives — just like teenagers.

Clouds of Dust and Gas

1) Stars <u>initially form</u> from clouds of <u>DUST AND GAS</u>.

Protostar

2) The <u>force of gravity</u> makes the dust particles come <u>spiralling in together</u>. As they do, <u>gravitational energy</u> is converted into <u>heat energy</u> and the <u>temperature rises</u>.

Main Sequence Star

3) When the <u>temperature</u> gets <u>high enough</u>, <u>hydrogen nuclei</u> undergo <u>nuclear fusion</u> to form <u>helium nuclei</u> and give out massive amounts of <u>heat and light</u>. A star is born. It immediately enters a long <u>stable period</u> in which the <u>heat created</u> by the nuclear fusion provides an <u>outward pressure</u> to <u>BALANCE</u> the <u>force of gravity</u> pulling everything <u>inwards</u>. The Sun's presently in the middle of its stable period, and luckily for us it's still got about <u>5 billion years</u> to go. (Or to put it another way, the <u>Earth's</u> already had <u>HALF its innings</u> before the Sun <u>engulfs</u> it!)

Red Giant

4) Eventually the <u>hydrogen</u> begins to <u>run out</u> and the star then <u>swells</u> into a <u>RED GIANT</u>. It becomes <u>red</u> because the surface <u>cools</u>. At this stage the Sun's surface will reach out to <u>past the Earth's present orbit</u>, and the Earth will be <u>swallowed up</u>. Still, at least it won't happen for a <u>few more billion years</u>...

5) A <u>SMALL STAR</u> like our Sun will then begin to <u>cool</u> and <u>contract</u> into a <u>WHITE DWARF</u>. The <u>matter</u> from which <u>white dwarfs</u> are made is <u>MILLIONS OF TIMES DENSER</u> than any matter on Earth because the <u>gravity is so strong</u> it even crushes the <u>atoms</u>. A white dwarf is about the <u>size of the Earth</u>, yet it contains virtually all the <u>mass</u> of the <u>original star</u>.

Big stars | Small stars

White Dwarf

Supernova

6) <u>BIG STARS</u> on the other hand will eventually <u>explode</u> in a <u>SUPERNOVA</u>, providing gas and dust to start the whole process again...

Twinkle twinkle little star, how I wond.. — JUST LEARN IT PAL...

Erm. Just how do they know all that? As if it's not outrageous enough that they reckon to know the whole history of the Earth for the last five billion years, they also reckon to know the whole life cycle of stars, when they're all billions and billions of km away. It's just an outrage.

SEG Syllabus

SECTION FOUR — THE EARTH & BEYOND

Revision Summary for Section Four

The Universe is completely mind-blowing in its own right. But surely the most mind-blowing thing of all is the very fact that we are actually here, sitting and contemplating the truly outrageous improbability of our own existence. If your mind isn't blowing, then it hasn't sunk in yet. Think about it. 15 billion years ago there was a huge explosion, but there was no need for the whole chain of events to happen that allowed (or caused?) intelligent life to evolve and develop to the point where it became conscious of its own existence, not to mention the very disturbing unlikelihood of it all. But we have. We're here. Maaaan — is that freaky or what? The Universe could so easily have existed without conscious life ever evolving. Or come to that, the Universe needn't exist at all. Just black nothingness. So why does it exist? And why are we here? And why do we have to do so much revision? Who knows — but stop dreaming and get on with it.

1) List the nine planets of the Solar System, and get them in the right order.
2) Which is the biggest planet? Which is the smallest? Sketch the relative sizes of all of them.
3) What's the big difference between planets and stars?
4) How does the Sun produce all its heat? What does the Sun give out?
5) What is it that keeps the planets in their orbits? What other things are held in orbits?
6) What are constellations? What do planets do in the constellations?
7) Who had trouble with the boys in the red robes? Why did he have such trouble?
8) Describe the differences between the old fashioned view of the Solar System and the one we have now.
9) What are asteroids? Between which two planets do most of them orbit?
10) What and where are comets? What are they made of? Sketch a diagram of a comet orbit.
11) Sketch a diagram to explain how day and night come about.
12) Which parts of the world have the longest days and which parts have the shortest days?
13) Sketch a diagram to show how the seasons come about.
14) How long does a full rotation of the Earth take? How long does a full orbit of the Sun take?
15) What's the difference between natural and artificial satellites?
16) Explain fully what a low polar orbit satellite does, and state what they're used for.
17) Explain fully what a geostationary satellite does, and state what they're used for.
18) Which of the two types of satellite takes longer to orbit the Earth? Explain why.
19) What is the Hubble Telescope and where is it? What's the big idea there then?
20) What is the Milky Way? Sketch it and show the Sun in relation to it.
21) What is the Universe made up of? How big is it?
22) What is a light year? How big is it?
23) What is the main theory of the origin of the Universe? Give brief details of the theory.
24) Describe an important piece of evidence for this theory.
25) Approximately how long ago did the Universe begin?
26) Describe the first stages of a star's formation. Where does the initial energy come from?
27) What process eventually starts inside the star to make it produce so much heat and light?
28) What are the final two stages of a small star's life?
29) How strange is the Universe? What's the most mind-blowing thing ever?

SECTION FOUR — THE EARTH & BEYOND

ENERGY RESOURCES & ENERGY TRANSFER

Sources of Power

Energy Resources

There are <u>eleven</u> different types of <u>energy resource</u> that you need to know about.
They fit into <u>two broad types</u>: <u>RENEWABLE</u> and <u>NON-RENEWABLE</u>.

Non-Renewable Energy Resources Will Run Out One Day

The <u>non-renewables</u> are the <u>THREE FOSSIL FUELS</u> and <u>NUCLEAR</u>:

1) <u>COAL</u>
2) <u>OIL</u>
3) <u>NATURAL GAS</u>
4) <u>NUCLEAR FUELS</u> (<u>uranium</u> and <u>plutonium</u>)

a) They will <u>ALL RUN OUT</u> one day.
b) They all do <u>DAMAGE</u> to the environment.
c) But they provide <u>MOST OF OUR ENERGY</u>.

Renewable Energy Resources Will Never Run Out

The <u>renewables</u> include:

1) <u>WIND POWER</u>
2) <u>WAVE POWER</u>
3) <u>TIDAL POWER</u>
4) <u>HYDROELECTRIC</u>
5) <u>SOLAR POWER</u>
6) <u>FOOD SUPPLIES</u>
7) <u>BIOMASS (ESPECIALLY WOOD)</u>

a) These will <u>NEVER RUN OUT</u>.
b) They <u>DO LITTLE DAMAGE TO THE ENVIRONMENT</u> (except visually).
c) The trouble is they <u>DON'T PROVIDE MUCH ENERGY</u> and many of them are <u>UNRELIABLE</u> because they depend on the <u>WEATHER</u>.

The Sun Is the Ultimate Source for Nine of the Energy Resources

(The exceptions are tide and nuclear — see below).
A useful way to show how energy is transferred from one medium to another is to draw an <u>energy transfer chain</u>. For most of our energy resources, these will start with the <u>Sun</u>.
Here's three examples that you need to know:

1) <u>Sun</u> ➡ <u>light energy</u> ➡ <u>photosynthesis</u> ➡ <u>dead plants/animals</u> ➡ <u>FOSSIL FUELS</u>.

2) <u>Sun</u> ➡ <u>heats atmosphere</u> ➡ <u>creates WINDS</u> ➡ <u>and therefore WAVES too</u>.

3) <u>Sun</u> ➡ <u>light energy</u> ➡ <u>SOLAR POWER</u>.

The Sun Generates Its Energy by Nuclear Fusion Reactions

1) <u>Hydrogen nuclei</u> near the Sun's centre fuse together to form <u>helium nuclei</u>.
2) This process releases <u>energy</u> — it is the ultimate source of the Sun's heat.
3) Some of this energy eventually reaches the Earth in the form of <u>EM waves</u> (mainly as <u>light and heat radiation</u>).

Higher

Nuclear and Tidal Energy Do NOT Originate in the Sun

1) <u>Nuclear power</u> comes from the energy <u>locked up</u> in the <u>nuclei of atoms</u>.
2) <u>Tides</u> are caused by the <u>gravitational attraction</u> of the <u>Moon</u> and the <u>Sun</u>.

Stop fuelling around and learn this stuff properly...

There's a lot of details here on sources of energy — an awful lot of details. Trouble is, in the Exam they could test you on any of them, so I guess you just gotta learn 'em.

SEG Syllabus   SECTION FIVE — ENERGY RESOURCES & ENERGY TRANSFER

Power from Non-Renewables

Energy Resources

MOST of the electricity we use is _generated_ from the four NON-RENEWABLE sources of energy (_coal_, _oil_, _gas_ and _nuclear_) in big power stations, which are all pretty much _the same_, apart from the _boiler_. LEARN the _basic features_ of the typical power station shown here:

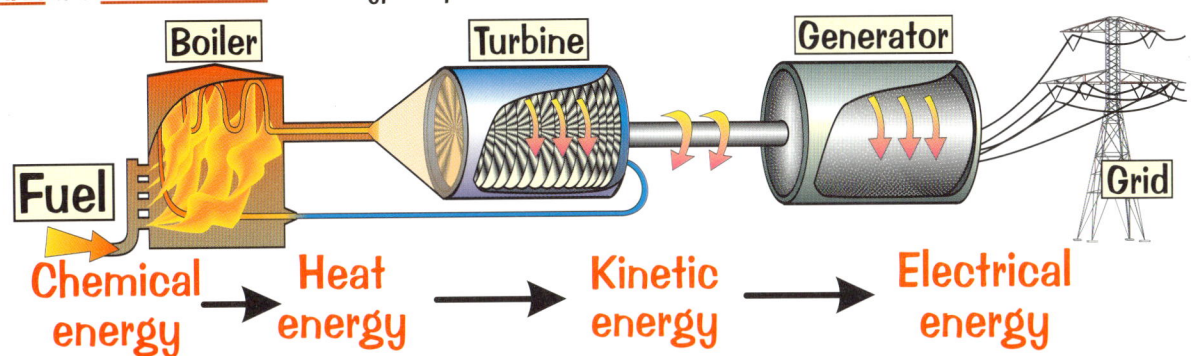

Boiler → Turbine → Generator → Grid

Fuel

Chemical energy → Heat energy → Kinetic energy → Electrical energy

Nuclear Reactors Are Just Fancy Boilers

1) A _nuclear power station_ is mostly the same as the one shown above, where _heat is produced_ in a _boiler_ to make _steam_ to drive the _turbines_, etc.
2) The only difference is in the _boiler_, which is just a tadge more _complicated_, as shown here:

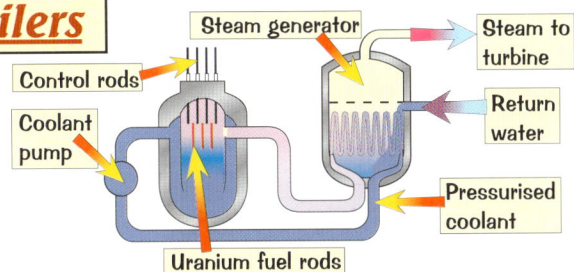

(Diagram labels: Steam generator, Steam to turbine, Control rods, Return water, Coolant pump, Pressurised coolant, Uranium fuel rods)

Comparison of Renewables and Non-Renewables

1) They're quite likely to give you an Exam question asking you to "_evaluate_" or "_discuss_" the _relative merits_ of generating power by _renewable_ and _non-renewable_ resources.
2) The way to get _good marks_ here is to simply list the _pros and cons_ for each method.
3) There are some _clear generalisations_ you should _definitely learn_ to help you answer such questions. Make sure you can _list those below from memory_. (See also the following pages, and esp. P. 73).

Non-Renewable Resources (Coal, Oil, Gas and Nuclear):

ADVANTAGES:
1) _High_ output.
2) _Reliable_ output.
3) They don't take up much _land_.
4) They can _match demand_ for power.

DISADVANTAGES:
1) Very _polluting_.
2) They involve _mining or drilling_ and then _transportation_ of fuels.
3) They are _running out_ quite quickly.
4) High cost of _building and de-commissioning_ of power stations.

Renewable Resources (Wind, Waves, Solar, Etc.):

ADVANTAGES:
1) _No pollution_.
2) _No fuel costs_.
(although the initial costs are high).

DISADVANTAGES:
1) Require _large areas of land_ or water and often _spoil the landscape_.
2) They don't always deliver _when needed_ — if the weather isn't right, for example.

Learn about the non-renewables — before it's too late...

Make sure you realise that we generate most of our electricity from the four non-renewables. The comparison bit's also pretty important — you've just gotta know the differences between renewable and non-renewable energy — or I hold out _no hope_ for you in the Exam...

SECTION FIVE — ENERGY RESOURCES & ENERGY TRANSFER   SEG SYLLABUS

Power from Renewables

Energy Resources

Wind Power — Lots of Little Wind Turbines

1) This involves putting lots of *windmills* (wind turbines) up in *exposed places*, like on *moors* or round *coasts*.
2) Each wind turbine has its own *generator* inside it, so the electricity is generated *directly* from the *wind* turning the *blades*.
3) There's *no pollution*.
4) But they do *spoil the view*. You need about *5,000 wind turbines* to replace one *coal-fired power station* and 5,000 of them cover *a lot* of ground — that wouldn't look very nice at all.
5) There's also the problem of *no power when the wind stops*, and it's *impossible* to *increase supply* when there's *extra demand*.
6) The initial costs are *quite high*, but there are *no* fuel costs and *minimal running costs*.

Solar Panels Use the Sun's Energy Directly

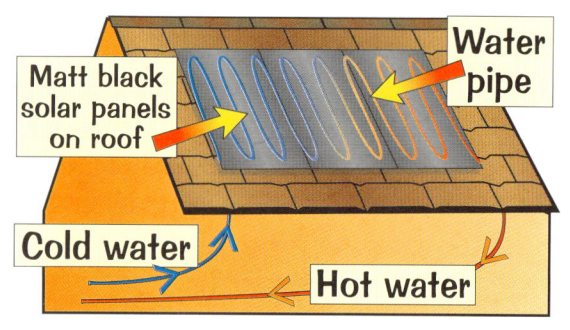

SOLAR PANELS are much less sophisticated than solar cells (like those that power some calculators). They simply contain *water pipes* under a *black surface*.

Heat radiation from the Sun is *absorbed* by the *black surface* to *heat the water* in the pipes. The hot water can then be used for a number of purposes, such as heating a home.

In sunny countries solar power is a *very reliable source* of energy — but only in the *daytime*. *Initial costs* can be *high*, but after that the energy is *free* and *running costs almost nil*. Solar panels cause *no pollution* in their operation.

Pumped Storage Gives Extra Supply Just When It's Needed

1) Most large power stations have *huge boilers* that have to be kept running *all night*, even though demand is *very low*. This means there's a *surplus* of electricity at night.
2) It's surprisingly *difficult* to find a way of *storing* this spare energy for *later use*.
3) *Pumped storage* is one of the *best solutions* to the problem.
4) In pumped storage "spare" *night-time electricity* is used to pump water up to a *higher* reservoir.
5) This can then be released *quickly* during periods of *peak* demand, such as at *tea time* each evening, to supplement the *steady delivery* from the big power stations.
6) Remember, *pumped storage ISN'T* a way of *generating* power — but simply a way of *storing energy* that has *already* been generated.

Learn about wind power — it can blow your mind...

Lots of important details here on all these nice green squeaky clean sources of energy. Perfect mini-essay material, I'd say. Three nice green squeaky clean *mini-essays* please. *Enjoy*.

SEG SYLLABUS — SECTION FIVE — ENERGY RESOURCES & ENERGY TRANSFER

Power from Renewables

Energy Resources

Don't confuse *wave power* with *tidal power*. They are *completely different*.

Wave Power — Lots of little Wave Machines

1) You need lots of small *wave generators* located *around the coast*.
2) As waves come in to the shore they provide an *up and down motion* which can be used to drive a *generator*.
3) There is *no* pollution. The main problems are *spoiling the view* and being a *hazard* to boats.
4) They are *fairly unreliable*, since waves tend to die out when the *wind drops*.
5) Initial costs are *high*, but there's *no fuel costs* and *minimal* running costs. Wave power is never likely to provide energy on a *large scale* but it can be *very useful* on *small islands*.

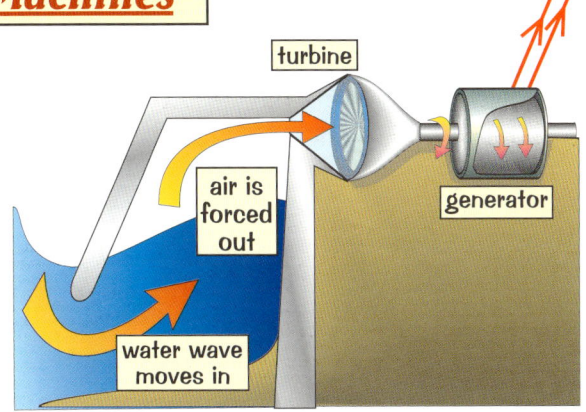

Tidal Barrages — Using the Sun and Moon's Gravity

1) *Tidal barrages* are *big dams* with *turbines* in them, built across places like river *estuaries*.
2) As the tide *comes in* it fills up the estuary to a height of *several metres*. This water can then be allowed out through *turbines* at a controlled speed. It also drives the turbines on the way in.
3) There is *no pollution*. The source of the energy is the gravity of the Sun and the Moon.
4) The main problems are *preventing free access* by boats, *spoiling* the view, and possibly *altering habitats* (although this is *not certain* since the tide comes *in and out anyway*).
5) Tides are pretty *reliable* in the sense that they happen *twice a day* without fail, and always to the *predicted height*. The only drawback is that the *height* of the tide is *variable*, so lower (neap) tides will provide significantly *less energy* than the bigger "*spring*" tides. But tidal barrages are excellent for *storing energy* ready for periods of *peak demand*.
6) *Initial costs* are *moderately high*, but there's *no fuel costs* and *minimal* running costs. Even though it can only be used in a *few* of the *most suitable* estuaries, tidal power has the potential for generating a *significant* amount of energy.

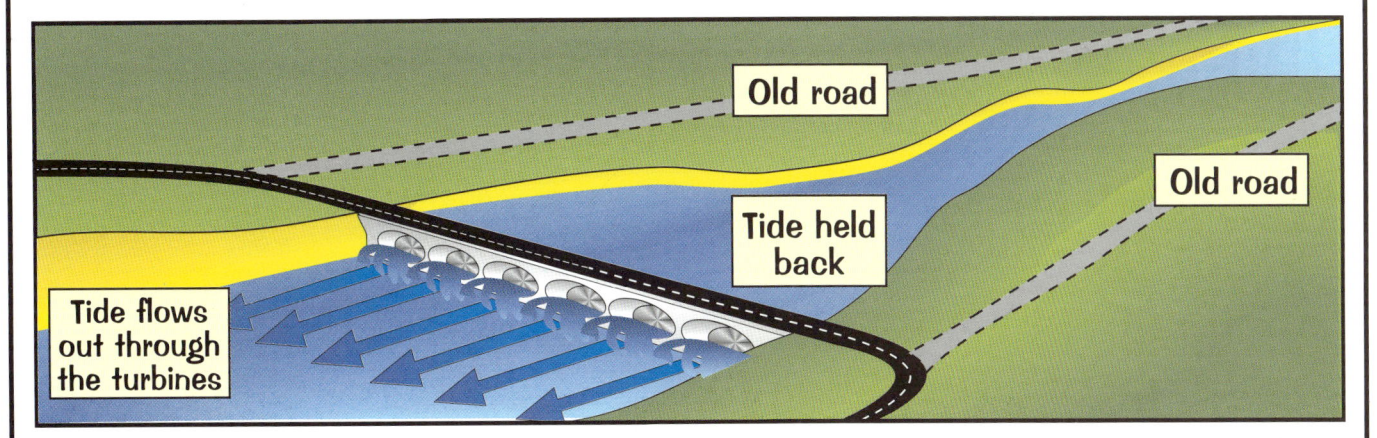

Once again, don't confuse *tidal power* with *wave power*. They are *completely different*.

Learn about wave power — and bid your cares goodbye...

I do hope you appreciate the big big differences between tidal power and wave power. They both involve salty sea water, sure — but there the similarities end. Lots of jolly details then, just waiting to be absorbed into your cavernous intra-cranial void. Smile and enjoy. And *learn*.

SECTION FIVE — ENERGY RESOURCES & ENERGY TRANSFER   SEG SYLLABUS

Types of Energy Transfer

Energy Transfers

Learn All the Ten Types of Energy

You should know all of these *well enough* to list them *from memory*, including the examples:
1) ELECTRICAL ENERGY........................... — whenever a current flows.
2) LIGHT ENERGY.................................... — from the Sun, light bulbs, etc.
3) SOUND ENERGY................................... — from loudspeakers or anything noisy.
4) KINETIC ENERGY, or MOVEMENT ENERGY.... — anything that's moving has it.
5) NUCLEAR ENERGY................................ — released only from nuclear reactions.
6) THERMAL ENERGY or HEAT ENERGY........... — flows from hot objects to colder ones.
7) RADIANT HEAT ENERGY, or INFRA RED HEAT — given out as EM radiation by hot objects.
8) GRAVITATIONAL POTENTIAL ENERGY........... — possessed by anything that can fall.
9) ELASTIC POTENTIAL ENERGY..................... — stretched springs, elastic, rubber bands, etc.
10) CHEMICAL ENERGY............................... — possessed by foods, fuels, batteries, etc.

Potential and Chemical Are Forms of Stored Energy

The *last three* above are forms of *stored energy* because the energy is not obviously *doing* anything — it's kind of *waiting to happen*, i.e. waiting to be turned into one of the *other* forms.

They Like Giving Exam Questions on Energy Transfers

These are *very important examples*. You must *learn them* till you can repeat them all *easily*.

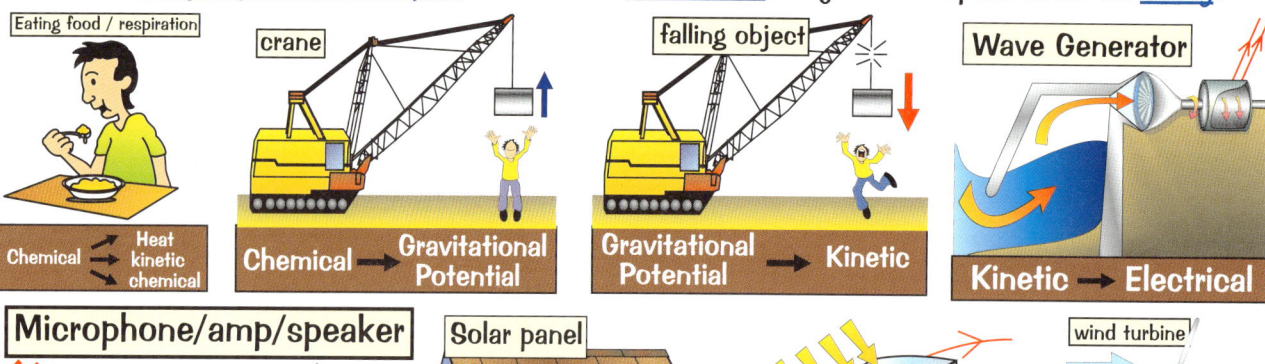

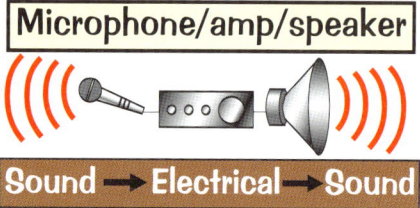

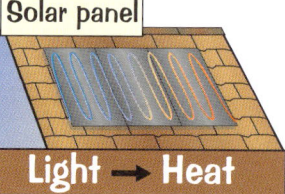

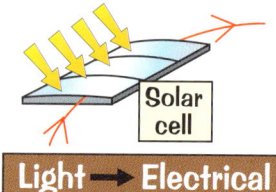

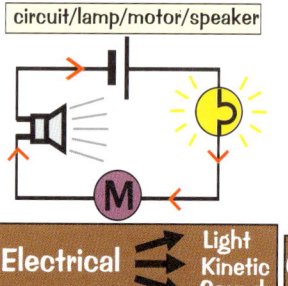

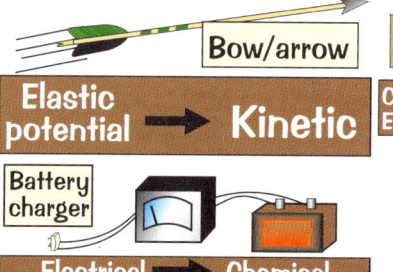

Eating food / respiration: Chemical ⇄ Heat, kinetic, chemical

crane: Chemical → Gravitational Potential

falling object: Gravitational Potential → Kinetic

Wave Generator: Kinetic → Electrical

Microphone/amp/speaker: Sound → Electrical → Sound

Solar panel: Light → Heat

Solar cell: Light → Electrical

wind turbine: Kinetic → Electrical

circuit/lamp/motor/speaker: Electrical ⇄ Light, Kinetic, Sound

Archer/bow: Chemical → Elastic potential

Bow/arrow: Elastic potential → Kinetic

Battery charger: Electrical → Chemical

JACK: Chemical → Elastic Potential; Elastic Potential → Kinetic

And DON'T FORGET — ALL types of ENERGY are measured in JOULES

Learn about energy — and just keep working at it...

They're pretty keen on the different types of energy and also energy transfers. You'll definitely get an Exam question on it, and if you learn all the stuff on this page, you should have it pretty well covered I'd think. *Learn, cover, scribble, check, learn, cover, scribble*, etc. etc.

SEG SYLLABUS — SECTION FIVE — ENERGY RESOURCES & ENERGY TRANSFER

Heat Transfer

Energy Transfers

There are _three_ distinct methods of heat transfer: _CONDUCTION_, _CONVECTION_ and _RADIATION_.
To answer Exam questions you _must_ use those _three key words_ in just the _right places_.
And that means you need to know _exactly what they are_, and all the _differences_ between them.

Heat Energy Causes Molecules to Move Faster

1) _Heat energy_ causes _gas and liquid_ molecules to move around _faster_, and causes particles in solids to vibrate _more rapidly_.
2) When particles move _faster_ it shows up as a _rise_ in temperature.
3) This extra _kinetic energy_ of the particles tends to get _dissipated_ to the _surroundings_.
4) In other words the _heat_ energy tends to flow _away_ from a hotter object to its _cooler_ surroundings. But then you knew that already. I would hope.

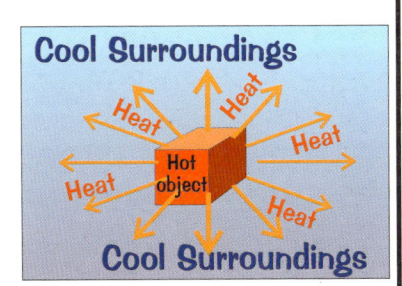

If there's a _DIFFERENCE IN TEMPERATURE_ between two places then _HEAT WILL FLOW_ between them.

Temperature Is Measured in Degrees Celsius (°C)

The _Celsius Temperature Scale_ cunningly defines _0°C_ to be the _melting point of water_, and _100°C_ to be its _boiling point_, just to make life easier for GCSE Physics students. How thoughtful...

Evaporation Is Another Way That Heat Can Be Lost

1) In a _liquid_ the _hottest_ particles are moving the _fastest_.
2) _Fast-moving_ particles near the liquid _surface_ are likely to _break free_ of the liquid and _evaporate_.
3) Only the _fastest_ particles will achieve this, leaving the _slower_, "_cooler_" particles _behind_.
4) This _lowers the average energy_ of the particles left in the liquid and so _the liquid as a whole_ becomes _cooler_.
5) It then _takes in heat_ from its surroundings and thereby _cools_ whatever it's in _contact_ with. This is how _sweating_ helps to cool the body.

You can _INCREASE_ the rate of _EVAPORATION_ from a liquid surface in _FOUR_ different ways:
   1) by increasing the _SURFACE AREA_ of the liquid (so _more particles_ are _near the surface_).
   2) by increasing the _TEMPERATURE_ of the liquid (so _more particles_ have _enough energy_ to leave the surface).
   3) by _DE_creasing the _HUMIDITY_ of the surrounding air (_drier air_ can _absorb more water_).
   4) by increasing the _MOVEMENT_ of the surrounding air (so the _wet air_ near the surface is _rapidly replaced_ by drier air).

Don't get hot under the collar — learn about evaporation...

OK, so there's two main sections here, and lots of colourful details to wedge into that brain of yours. Evaporation's particularly tricky — you really do need to know all those numbered points. So what are you waiting for — _cover the page_ and write down those _mini-essays_.

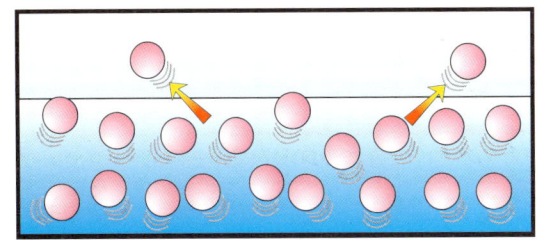

SECTION FIVE — ENERGY RESOURCES & ENERGY TRANSFER   SEG Syllabus

Conduction of Heat

Energy Transfers

Conduction of Heat — Occurs Mainly in Solids

HOT → HEAT FLOW → **COLD**

CONDUCTION OF HEAT is the process in which **VIBRATING PARTICLES** pass on their **EXTRA VIBRATIONAL ENERGY** to **NEIGHBOURING PARTICLES**.

This process continues _throughout the solid_, and gradually the _extra vibrational energy_ (or _heat_) is passed all the way through the solid, causing a _rise in temperature_ at the other side.

Non-Metals Are Good Insulators

1) This normal process of _conduction_ (as illustrated above) is always _very slow_.
2) But in most _non-metal solids_ it's the _only_ way that heat can pass through.
3) So _non-metals_ (such as _plastic_, _wood_, _rubber_, etc.) are very good _insulators_.
4) Non-metal _gases and liquids_ are even _worse conductors_, as you will slowly begin to realise if I say it often enough. Metals, on the other hand, are a totally different ball game...

All Metals Are Good Conductors Due to Their Free Electrons

HOT → Heat carried in metals by the free electrons → **COLD**

1) _Metals_ "_conduct_" so well because the electrons are _free to move_ inside the metal.
2) At the _hot end_ the electrons move _faster_ and diffuse _more quickly_ through the metal.
3) So the electrons carry their _energy_ quite a _long way_ before _giving it up_ in a _collision_.
4) This is obviously a much _faster way_ of _transferring_ the energy through the metal than slowly passing it between jostling _neighbouring_ atoms. This is why _heat_ travels so _fast_ through _metals_.

Metals Always FEEL Hotter or Colder Because They Conduct So Well

You'll notice if a _spade_ is left out in the _sun_ that the _metal part_ will always _feel_ much _hotter_ than the _wooden_ handle. But _IT ISN'T HOTTER_ — it just _conducts_ the heat into your hand much quicker than the wood, so your hand _heats up_ much quicker.
In _cold weather_, the _metal bits_ of a spade, or anything else, always _feel colder_ because they _take the heat away_ from your hand quicker. But they're _NOT COLDER_... Remember that.

Good conductors are always metals? — what about Henry Wood...

Here's a little joker with which to amaze and entertain your family and friends at Christmas: the only reason metals are such good "conductors" is because the free electrons _convect_ the heat through the metal. Is it true? Answers on a post card. _Learn this page_ then _cover and scribble_.

SEG SYLLABUS — SECTION FIVE — ENERGY RESOURCES & ENERGY TRANSFER

Convection of Heat

Energy Transfers

Gases and liquids are usually free to *slosh about* — and that allows them to transfer heat by *convection*, which is a *much more effective process* than conduction.

Convection of Heat — Liquids and Gases Only

Convection simply *can't happen in solids* because the particles *can't move*.

CONVECTION occurs when the more energetic particles **MOVE** from a *hotter region* to a *cooler region* — **AND TAKE THEIR HEAT ENERGY WITH THEM.**

Once they have reached the cooler region, the *more energetic* (i.e. *hotter*) particles *transfer their energy* by the usual process of *collisions* — warming up the surroundings.

Natural Convection Currents Are Caused by Changes in Density

The diagram shows a *typical convection current*. Make sure you *learn* all the bits about *expansion* and *density changes* which *cause* the convection current. It's all worth *juicy marks* in the Exam.

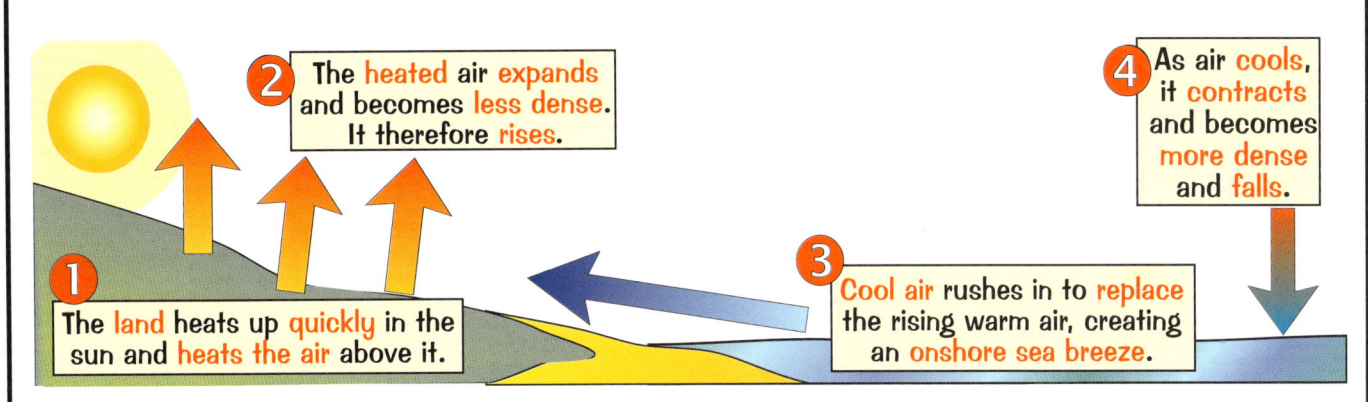

1 The land heats up quickly in the sun and heats the air above it.

2 The heated air expands and becomes less dense. It therefore rises.

3 Cool air rushes in to replace the rising warm air, creating an onshore sea breeze.

4 As air cools, it contracts and becomes more dense and falls.

Natural Convection Produces Ocean Currents

1) The ocean near the *Equator* is heated *most strongly* by the Sun. The warmed water *expands* slightly, pushing outwards both north and south. It is replaced by colder water *rising up* from underneath, which is then heated. The resulting warm *surface currents* can travel for *hundreds of miles*.

2) The same thing happens in a beaker, but on a smaller scale.

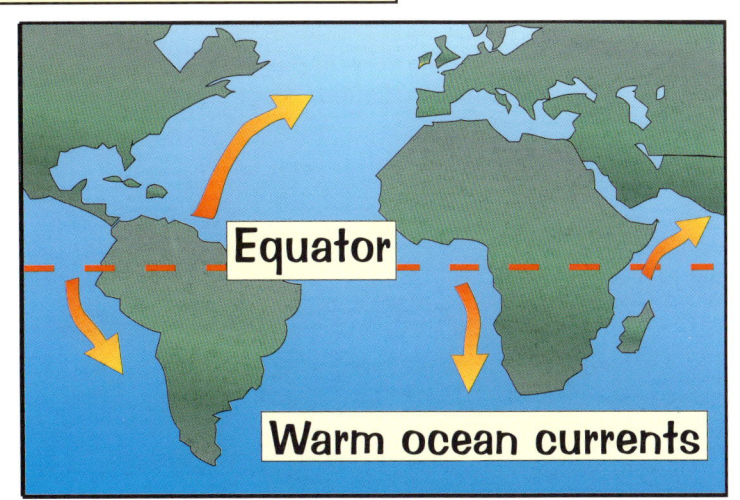

Equator

Warm ocean currents

Convection currents — easy as a summer evening breeze...

Watch out — it's another pair of Physics words that look so much alike that half of you think they're the same word. Look: CON**VEC**TION. See, it's different from CON**DUC**TION. Tricky that one isn't it. Just like ref**lec**tion and ref**rac**tion. Not just a different word though, convection is a *totally different process* too. Make sure you learn exactly why it isn't like conduction.

SECTION FIVE — ENERGY RESOURCES & ENERGY TRANSFER   SEG SYLLABUS

Heat Radiation

Energy Transfers

Heat radiation can also be called infrared radiation, and it consists purely of electromagnetic waves. It's just below visible light in the electromagnetic spectrum.

Heat Radiation Can Travel Through a Vacuum

Heat radiation is different from the other two methods of heat transfer in quite a few ways:
1) It travels in straight lines at the speed of light.
2) It travels through a vacuum. This is the only way that heat can reach us from the Sun.
3) It can be very effectively reflected by a silver surface.
4) It only travels through transparent media, like air, glass and water.
5) Its behaviour is strongly dependent on surface colour and texture. This definitely isn't so for conduction and convection.

Emission and Absorption of Heat Radiation

1) All objects are continually emitting and absorbing heat radiation.
2) The hotter they are, the more heat radiation they emit.
3) Cooler objects around them will absorb this heat radiation. You can feel this heat radiation if you stand near something hot like a fire.

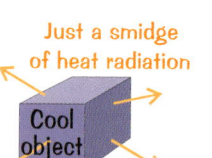

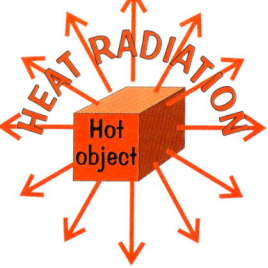

Carbon dioxide (CO_2) absorbs low energy infrared, but lets higher energy infrared pass through. This means that the Sun's radiation will mostly reach the Earth's surface, but heat emitted from the Earth tends to be absorbed by the atmosphere, from where it is often re-radiated back to the surface. So the more CO_2 there is in the atmosphere, the warmer the Earth gets. This is known as the GREENHOUSE EFFECT.

It Depends an Awful Lot on Surface Colour and Texture

1) Dark matt surfaces ABSORB heat radiation falling on them much more strongly than bright glossy surfaces, such as gloss white or silver. They also emit heat radiation much more too.
2) Silvered surfaces REFLECT nearly all heat radiation falling on them.
3) In the lab there are several fairly dull experiments to demonstrate the effects of surface on emission and absorption of heat radiation. Here are two of the most gripping:

Leslie's Cube

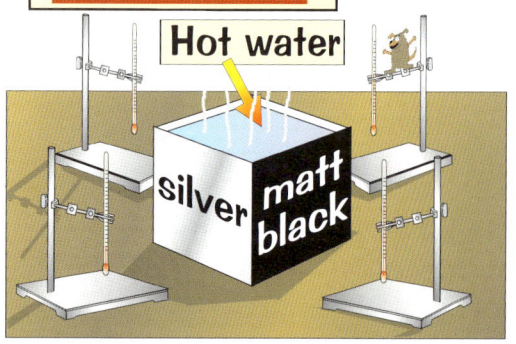

The matt black side EMITS most heat, so it's that thermometer which gets hottest.

The matt black surface ABSORBS most heat, so its wax melts first and the ball bearing drops.

The Melting Wax Trick

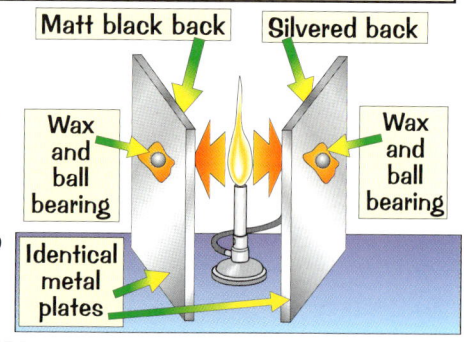

Revise heat radiation — absorb as much as you can...

The main thing to learn here is that heat radiation is strongly affected by the colour and texture of surfaces. Don't forget that the other two types of heat transfer, conduction and convection, are not affected by surface colour and texture at all. Heat radiation is totally different from conduction and convection. Learn all the details on this page, then cover it up and scribble.

SEG SYLLABUS — SECTION FIVE — ENERGY RESOURCES & ENERGY TRANSFER

Heat Transfer Summary

Conduction, Convection and Radiation Compared

These differences are really important — make sure you *LEARN them*:

1) *Conduction* occurs mainly in *solids*.
2) *Convection* occurs mainly in *gases and liquids*.
3) Gases and liquids are *very poor conductors* — convection is usually the *dominant* process. Where convection *can't* occur, the heat transfer by *conduction* is *very slow* indeed.
4) *Radiation* travels through anything *see-through*, including a *vacuum*.
5) *Heat radiation* is given out by *anything* that is *warm or hot*.
6) The *amount* of heat radiation which is *absorbed or emitted* depends on the *colour* and *texture* of the *surface*. But don't forget, *convection* and *conduction* are totally *unaffected* by surface colour or texture. A *shiny white* surface *conducts* just as well as a *matt black* one.

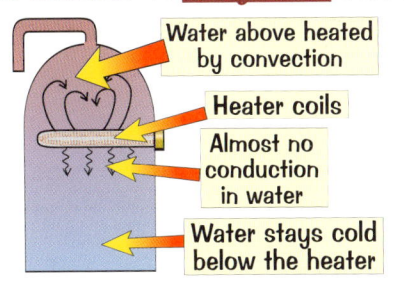

- Water above heated by convection
- Heater coils
- Almost no conduction in water
- Water stays cold below the heater

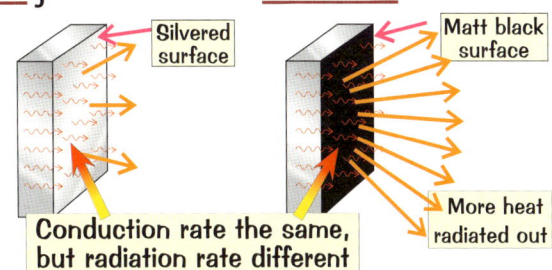

- Silvered surface
- Matt black surface
- Conduction rate the same, but radiation rate different
- More heat radiated out

Good Conductors and Good Insulators

1) *All metals* are *good* conductors e.g. iron, brass, aluminium, copper, gold, silver etc.
2) All *non-metals* are good *insulators*.
3) Gases and liquids are truly *abysmal conductors* (but are great *convectors* don't forget).
4) The *best* insulators are ones that trap *pockets of air*. If the air *can't move*, it *can't* transfer heat by *convection*, and so the heat has to *conduct* very slowly through the *pockets of air*, as well as the material in between. This really slows it down *big style*.
   This is how *clothes* and *blankets* and *loft insulation* and *cavity wall insulation* and *polystyrene cups* and *pretty woollen mittens* and *little furry animals* and *fluffy yellow ducklings* work.

Insulation Should Also Take Account of Heat Radiation

1) *Silvered finishes* are highly effective *insulation* against heat transfer by *radiation*.
2) This can work *both ways*, either keeping heat radiation *out* or keeping heat *in*.

KEEPING HEAT RADIATION OUT:	KEEPING HEAT IN:
Spacesuits	Shiny metal kettles
Cooking foil on the turkey	Survival blankets
Vacuum flasks	Vacuum flasks (again)

3) *Matt black* is rarely used for its thermal properties of *absorbing* and *emitting* heat radiation.
4) It's only *useful* where you want to *get rid of heat*, e.g. the *cooling fins* or *radiator* on an engine.

Learn the facts on heat transfer — but don't get a sweat on...

Phew, no more numbers and formulae — now we're back to good old straightforward factual learning again. Much less confusing — but no less of a challenge, it has to be said. You've really got to make a fair old effort to get those three key processes of heat transfer all sorted out in your head so that you know exactly what they are and when they occur. *Learn and grin*.

SECTION FIVE — ENERGY RESOURCES & ENERGY TRANSFER   SEG SYLLABUS

Applications of Heat Transfer

Energy Transfers

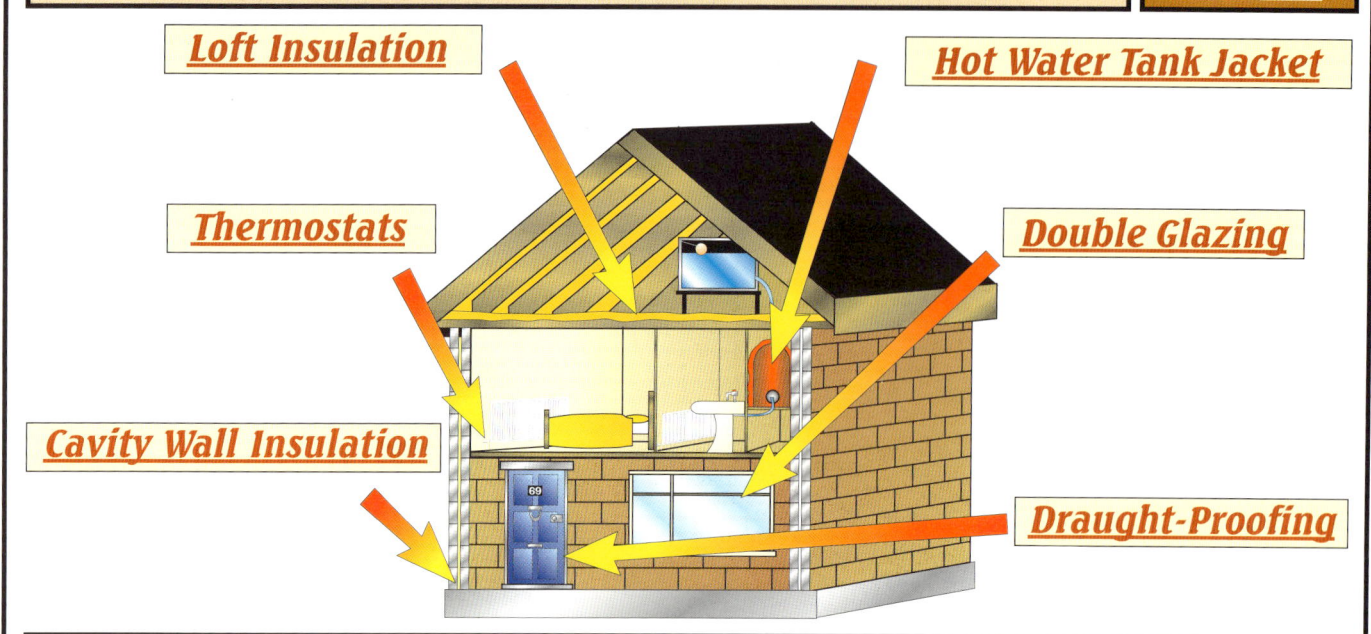

- Loft Insulation
- Hot Water Tank Jacket
- Thermostats
- Double Glazing
- Cavity Wall Insulation
- Draught-Proofing

Know Which Types of Heat Transfer Are Involved:

1) **CAVITY WALL INSULATION** — foam squirted into the gap between the bricks reduces *convection* and *radiation* across the gap.
2) **LOFT INSULATION** — a thick layer of fibreglass wool laid out across the whole loft floor reduces *conduction* and *radiation* into the roof space.
3) **DRAUGHT-PROOFING** — strips of foam and plastic around doors and windows stop draughts of cold air blowing in, i.e. they reduce heat loss due to *convection*.
4) **DOUBLE GLAZING** — two layers of glass with an air gap reduce *conduction* and *radiation*.
5) **THERMOSTATS ON RADIATOR VALVES** — these simply prevent the house being *over-warmed*.
6) **HOT WATER TANK JACKET** — lagging such as fibreglass wool reduces *conduction* and *radiation* from the hot water tank.
7) **THICK CURTAINS** — big bits of cloth you pull across the window to stop people looking in at you — but also to reduce heat loss by *conduction* and *radiation*.

The Vacuum Flask — the Ultimate in Insulation

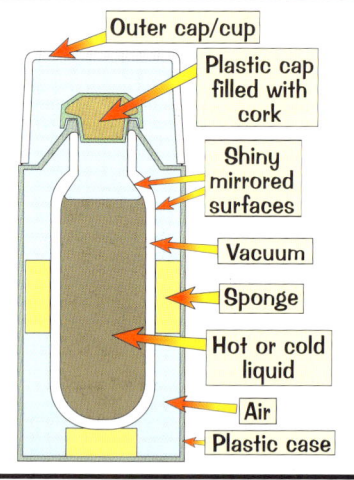

Labels: Outer cap/cup, Plastic cap filled with cork, Shiny mirrored surfaces, Vacuum, Sponge, Hot or cold liquid, Air, Plastic case

1) The glass bottle is *double-walled*, with a *thin vacuum* between the two walls. This stops *all conduction* and *convection* through the *sides*.
2) The walls either side of the vacuum are *silvered* to keep heat loss by *radiation* to a *minimum*.
3) The bottle is supported with *insulating foam*. This minimises heat *conduction* to or from the *outer* glass bottle.
4) The *stopper* is made from *plastic* and filled with *cork* or *foam* to reduce any *heat conduction* through it.

In *Exam questions* you must *always* say which form of heat transfer is involved at any point — either *conduction*, *convection* or *radiation*. "*The vacuum stops heat getting out*" will get you *no marks at all*.

Heat transfer and insulation — keep taking it all in...

There's a lot more to insulation than you first realise. That's because there are *three ways* that heat can be transferred, and so effective heat insulation has to deal with *all three*, of course. The venerable vacuum flask is the classic example of all-in-one-full-blown insulation. *Learn it*.

SEG Syllabus — SECTION FIVE — ENERGY RESOURCES & ENERGY TRANSFER

Useful Energy Transfers

Energy Transfers

Most Energy Transfers Involve Some Loss as Heat

Energy is ONLY USEFUL when it's CONVERTED from one form to another.

1) *Useful devices* are only *useful* because they *convert* energy from *one form* to *another*.
2) In doing so, some of the useful *input energy* is always *lost or wasted* as *heat*.
3) The *less energy* that is *wasted*, the *more efficient* the device is said to be.
4) The energy flow diagram is pretty much the same for *all devices*. You MUST learn this BASIC ENERGY FLOW DIAGRAM:

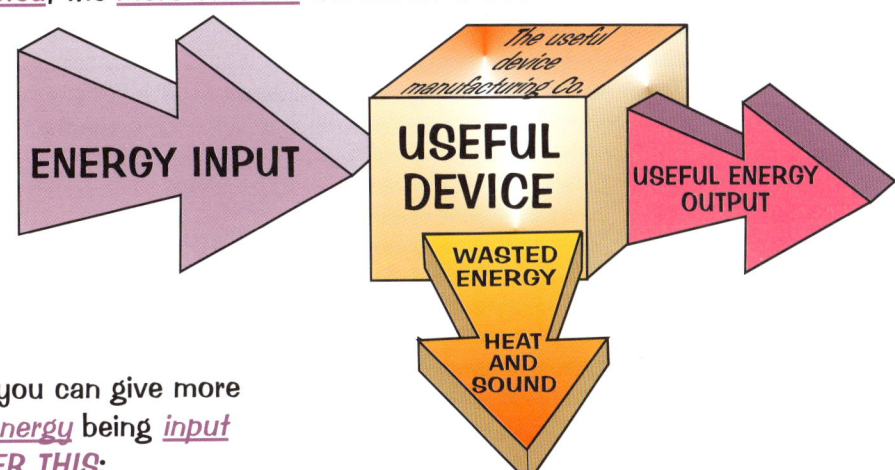

For any *specific example* you can give more detail about the *types of energy* being *input* and *output*, but REMEMBER THIS:

NO device is 100% efficient, and the WASTED ENERGY is always *dissipated* as HEAT and SOUND.

Electric heaters are kind of an *exception* to this. They could be considered *100% efficient* because *all* the electricity is converted to *"useful"* heat. *What else could it become?* Ultimately, *all* energy ends up as *heat energy*. If you use an electric drill, it gives out *various types* of energy, but they all quickly end up as *heat*. The wasted energy *and* the useful energy both end up just *warming the air* around us. This energy very quickly *spreads out* into the surroundings, and then it becomes harder and harder for us to use for further energy transfers. That's an important thing to realise. So realise it — and *never forget it*.

Don't Waste Energy — Don't Switch Anything On

Make sure you know all these easy examples — one of them is *bound* to come up in your Exams.

Device	Energy Input	Useful Output	Wasted Energy
1) Television	Electrical	Light and Sound	Heat
2) Light bulb	Electrical	Light	Heat
3) Electric drill	Electrical	Movement	Heat and Sound
4) Hairdrier	Electrical	Heat + movement	Heat and Sound
5) Car engine	Chemical	Movement	Heat and Sound
6) Horse	Chemical	Movement and ...	Heat and Sound

Learn about energy dissipation — but keep your cool...

The thing about loss of energy is it's always the same — it always disappears as heat and sound, and even the sound ends up as heat pretty quickly. So when they ask "Why is the input energy more than the output energy?", the answer is always the same... *Learn and enjoy*.

SECTION FIVE — ENERGY RESOURCES & ENERGY TRANSFER   SEG SYLLABUS

Efficiency of Machines

Energy Transfers

A *machine* is a device which turns *one type of energy* into *another*.
The *efficiency* of any device is defined as:

Efficiency = USEFUL Energy OUTPUT / TOTAL Energy INPUT

$$\frac{\text{Energy out}}{\text{Efficiency} \times \text{Energy in}}$$

You can give efficiency as a *fraction*, *decimal* or *percentage*, i.e. ¾ or 0.75 or 75%.

Come On! — Efficiency Is Really Simple...

1) You find how much energy is *supplied* to a machine. (The Total Energy *INPUT*)
2) You find how much *useful energy* the machine *delivers* (The Useful Energy *OUTPUT*)
   They either tell you this directly or they tell you how much it *wastes* as heat/sound.
3) Either way, you get those *two important numbers* and then just *divide* the *smaller one* by the *bigger one* to get a value for *efficiency* somewhere between *0 and 1* (or *0 and 100%*). Easy.
4) The other way they might ask it is to tell you the *efficiency* and the *input energy* and ask for the *energy output*. The best way to tackle that is to *learn* this *other version* of the formula:

USEFUL ENERGY OUTPUT = Efficiency × TOTAL Energy INPUT

Five Important Examples on Efficiency for You to Learn

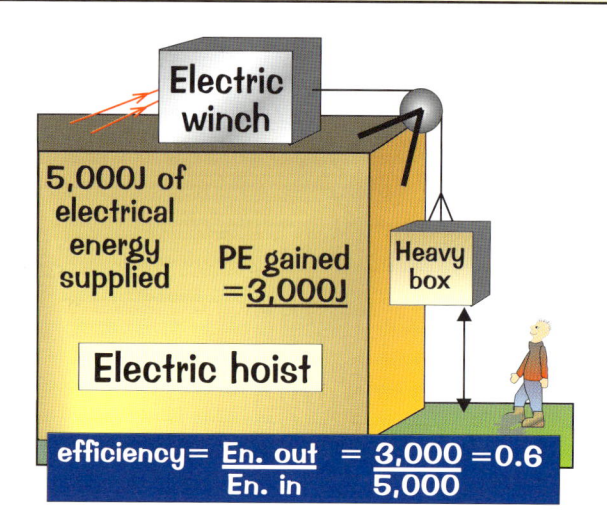

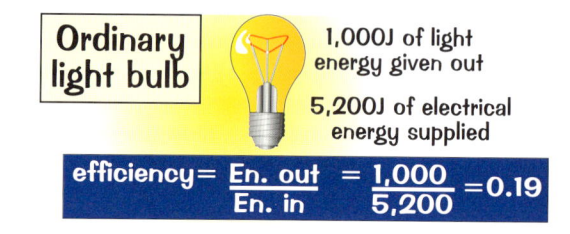

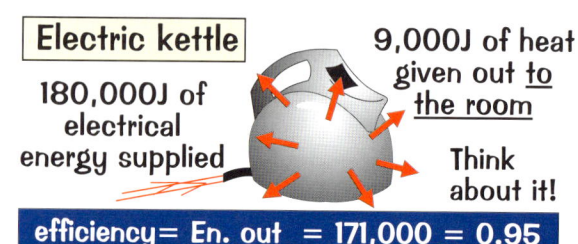

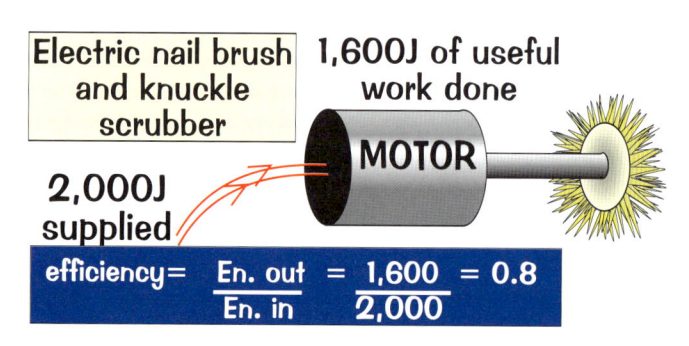

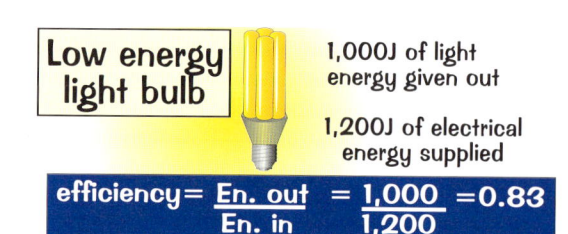

Electric hoist — Electric winch, 5,000J of electrical energy supplied, PE gained = 3,000J, Heavy box
efficiency = En. out / En. in = 3,000 / 5,000 = 0.6

Electric nail brush and knuckle scrubber — 2,000J supplied, MOTOR, 1,600J of useful work done
efficiency = En. out / En. in = 1,600 / 2,000 = 0.8

Ordinary light bulb — 1,000J of light energy given out, 5,200J of electrical energy supplied
efficiency = En. out / En. in = 1,000 / 5,200 = 0.19

Electric kettle — 180,000J of electrical energy supplied, 9,000J of heat given out to the room. Think about it!
efficiency = En. out / En. in = 171,000 / 180,000 = 0.95

Low energy light bulb — 1,000J of light energy given out, 1,200J of electrical energy supplied
efficiency = En. out / En. in = 1,000 / 1,200 = 0.83

Learn about energy transfer — but do it efficiently...

Efficiency is another hideously simple concept. It's a big funny-looking word I grant you, but that doesn't mean it's tricky. Let's face it, efficiency's a blummin' doddle — divide E_{out} by E_{in} and there it is, done. Geesh. *Learn the page*, then *cover it up* and *scribble down* what you know.

SEG Syllabus — SECTION FIVE — ENERGY RESOURCES & ENERGY TRANSFER

Energy Conservation

Energy Transfers

Non-Renewables Are Finite Resources

1) We don't have *unlimited supplies* of the *non-renewable* energy sources — especially *fossil fuels*. These fuels are therefore called *"finite"* resources (as opposed to *"infinite"*).
2) If we keep using them at the *present rate*, they'll soon *run out*. Well, soonish anyway.
3) Current known reserves for *oil* will only last us around *30 years*, while the known *gas* and *coal* reserves will last maybe *100* and *300* years respectively, if used at their *current rate*.
4) Of course more reserves will be found, but as we have already used the more convenient reserves, they're likely to be in *remote areas* or *deep underground*.
5) The increased difficulty in obtaining the fuels means that they will become *increasingly expensive* as the *supplies dwindle*.
6) Sooner or later we'll have to *stop using fossil fuels* — so the sooner we *develop the alternatives*, the better.

Environmental Problems with the Use of Non-Renewables

1) The burning of *all three fossil fuels* (coal, oil and gas) releases *carbon dioxide* (CO_2), which is increasing the *Greenhouse Effect* (see P. 68). This is almost certain to lead to *climate change* — and there's good evidence that it's *already started*.
2) The burning of *coal* and *oil* also causes *acid rain*. This is now being reduced by cleaning up the *emissions* — for example by the use of *electrostatic smoke precipitators* (see P. 2).
3) *Coal mining* makes a *mess* of the *landscape*, especially *"open-cast mining"*.
4) *Oil spillages* cause serious *environmental problems*. We try to avoid it, but it'll *always happen*.
5) *Nuclear power* is clean but the *nuclear waste* is very *dangerous* and difficult to *dispose of*.
6) Nuclear *fuel* (e.g. uranium) is *cheap* but the *overall cost* of nuclear power is *high* due to the cost of the *power plant* and final *decommissioning*.
7) *Nuclear power* always carries the risk of a *major catastrophe* like the *Chernobyl disaster*.

The Non-Renewables Need to Be Conserved

1) When the *fossil fuels* eventually *RUN OUT* we will *have* to use *other forms* of energy.
2) More importantly though is the question of whether we can *afford* to use all the fossil fuels, given their *effects on the environment*. It might be better to stop *BEFORE* they run out, and not leave it to *future generations* to clean up *our* mess.
3) There is a *general principle* of conservation that *all* people, both now and in the future, should have a *fair and appropriate share* of the *Earth's resources*.
4) It's mainly *first world countries* like *Britain* and the *US* that are using all the *fossil fuels*, so it's up to us to start using less of them. The US in particular emits about a *quarter* of the world's CO_2, yet it has just *4% of the population*.
5) To stop the fossil fuels *running out so quickly*, there are *two things* we can do:

1) Use Less Energy by Being More Efficient with It:

(i) Better *insulation* of buildings,
(ii) Turning *lights and other things OFF* when not needed,
(iii) Making everyone drive *spiddly little cars* with dippy little engines.

2) Use More of the Renewable Sources of Energy

There's loads of *renewable energy resources* just *screaming out* to be used and *further developed*. See pages 62 and 63 for details.

It's all doom and gloom — and that's just the weather...

This page is a bit wordy, I have to say. But all this stuff's in the syllabus, so you'd better learn it real good. There's four main sections here, which just happen to be perfect mini-essay material. So *learn the points, cover them up, scribble them down* — surely you know the drill by now...

SECTION FIVE — ENERGY RESOURCES & ENERGY TRANSFER   SEG SYLLABUS

Work Done, Energy and Power

Work, Power and Energy

When a *force* moves an *object*, ENERGY IS TRANSFERRED and WORK IS DONE.

That statement sounds far more complicated than it needs to. Try this:

1) Whenever something *moves*, something else is providing some sort of "*effort*" to move it.
2) The thing putting the *effort* in needs a *supply* of energy (like *fuel* or *food* or *electricity*, etc.).
3) It then does "*work*" by *moving* the object — and one way or another it *transfers* the energy it receives (as fuel) into *other forms*.
4) Whether this energy is transferred "*usefully*" (e.g. by *lifting a load*) or is "*wasted*" (e.g. lost as *friction*), you can still say that "*work is done*". Just like Batman and Bruce Wayne, "*work done*" and "*energy transferred*" are indeed "*one and the same*". (And they're both in *joules*).

It's Just Another Trivial Formula:

Work Done = Force × Distance

$$Wd = F \times d$$

Whether the force is *friction* or *weight* or *tension in a rope*, it's always the same. To find how much *energy* has been *transferred* (in joules), you just multiply the *force in N* by the *distance moved in m*. Easy as that. I'll show you...

EXAMPLE: Some hooligan kids drag an old tractor tyre 5m over rough ground. They pull with a total force of 340N. Find the energy transferred.
ANSWER: Wd = F×d = 340 × 5 = <u>1,700J</u>. Phew — easy peasy isn't it?

Power Is the "Rate of Doing Work" — I.e. How Much Per Second

POWER is *not* the same thing as *force*, nor *energy*. A *powerful* machine is not necessarily one that can exert a strong *force* (though it usually ends up that way).
A POWERFUL machine is one that transfers *A LOT OF ENERGY IN A SHORT SPACE OF TIME*. This is the *very easy formula* for power:

$$\text{Power} = \frac{\text{Work done}}{\text{Time taken}}$$

$$P \times t = Wd$$

EXAMPLE: A motor transfers 4.8kJ of useful energy in 2 minutes. Find its power output.
ANSWER: P = Wd / t = 4,800/120 = <u>40W</u> (or 40 J/s)
(Note that the kJ had to be turned into J, and the minutes into seconds.)

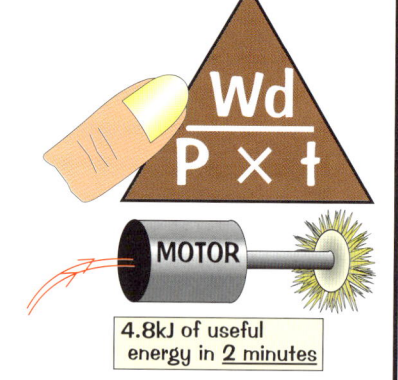

Power Is Measured in Watts (or J/s)

The proper unit of power is the *watt*. One watt = 1 joule of energy transferred per second. *Power* means "how much energy *per second*", so *watts* are the same as "*joules per second*" (J/s). Don't ever say "watts per second" — it's *nonsense*.

Revise work done — what else...

"*Energy transferred*" and "*work done*" are the same thing. I wonder how many times I need to say that before you'll remember. Power is "*work done divided by time taken*". I wonder how many times you've got to see that before you realise you're supposed to *learn it* as well...

SEG SYLLABUS — SECTION FIVE — ENERGY RESOURCES & ENERGY TRANSFER

Kinetic and Potential Energy

Work, Power and Energy

Kinetic Energy Is Energy of Movement

1) Anything that is _moving_ has _kinetic energy_.
2) The _kinetic energy_ of something depends both on its _MASS_ and _SPEED_.
3) The _more_ it weighs and the _faster_ it's going, the _greater_ its kinetic energy will be.
4) That's why the _stopping distance_ for a _fast car_ is much _greater_ than that for a _slow car_ — the faster car has to lose far more kinetic energy before it comes to a halt.

There's a _slightly tricky_ formula for it, so you have to concentrate _a little bit harder_ for this one. But hey, that's life — it can be real tough sometimes:

Kinetic Energy = ½ × mass × velocity²

$$K.E. = \frac{1}{2} \times m \times v^2$$

EXAMPLE: A car of mass 2,450kg is travelling at 38m/s. Calculate its kinetic energy.

ANSWER: It's pretty easy. You just plug the numbers into the formula — but watch the "v²"!
$KE = \frac{1}{2} m v^2 = \frac{1}{2} \times 2450 \times 38^2 = \underline{1,768,900J}$ (_joules_ because it's _energy_)

(When the car stops suddenly, all this energy is dissipated as heat at the brakes — it's a lot of heat)

- small mass, not fast low kinetic energy
- big mass, real fast high kinetic energy

Elastic Potential Energy Is Energy Stored in Springs

Elastic potential energy is the energy _stored_ when _work is done on an object_ to distort it. If a spring is either _compressed or stretched_, then it is said to have _elastic potential energy_.

Gravitational Potential Energy Is Energy Due to Height

Gravitational potential energy is the energy _stored in an object_ because it has been raised to a specific height _against_ the force of gravity.

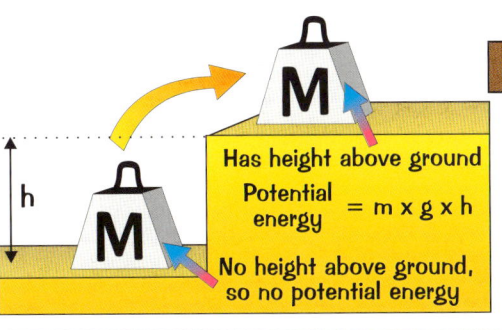

Potential Energy = mass × g × height

$$P.E. = m \times g \times h$$

- Has height above ground — Potential energy = m × g × h
- No height above ground, so no potential energy

Quite often _gravitational potential energy_ is just called "_potential energy_", but you should really use its full name. The proper name for g is "_gravitational field strength_". _On Earth_ this has the value of _g = 10m/s² (N/kg)_.

Kinetic energy — just get a move on and learn it, OK...

Phew! A couple of tricky formulae here. I mean gosh they've got more than three letters in them. Still, at least they fit into formula triangles, so you may still have some small chance of getting them right. Come on, I'm joking. Formulae are always _a doddle_, aren't they?

SECTION FIVE — ENERGY RESOURCES & ENERGY TRANSFER   SEG Syllabus

K.E. and P.E. — Some Examples

Work, Power and Energy

1) Working Out Potential Energy

EXAMPLE: A sheep of mass 47kg is slowly raised through 6.3m. Find the gain in potential energy.

ANSWER: This is pretty easy.
You just plug the numbers into the formula:
PE = mgh = 47 × 10 × 6.3 = **2,961J**
(*joules* again because it's *energy* again.)

What do you call a sheep with no eyes and no legs? Dunno? A Cloud!

2) Calculating Your Power Output

Both cases use the same formula:

$$\text{POWER} = \frac{\text{ENERGY TRANSFERRED}}{\text{TIME TAKEN}} \quad \text{or} \quad P = \frac{E}{t}$$

a) The Timed Run Upstairs:

In this case the "*energy transferred*" is simply the *potential energy you gain* (= mgh).
Hence **POWER = mgh/t**

62kg, 12m, Time taken = 14s

Power output
= En. transferred/time
= mgh/t
= (62 × 10 × 12) ÷ 14
= **531W**

b) The Timed Acceleration:

This time the *energy transferred* is the *kinetic energy you gain* (= ½mv²).
Hence **POWER = ½mv²/t**

62kg, 0 → 8m/s, time taken = 4s

Power output
= En. transferred/time
= ½mv²/t
= (½ × 62 × 8²) ÷ 4
= **496W**

3) Calculating the Speed of Falling Objects

When something falls, its *potential energy* is *converted* into *kinetic energy*.
Hence the *further* it falls, the *faster* it goes.
In practice, some of the PE will be *dissipated* as *heat* due to *air resistance*, but in Exam questions they'll likely say you can *ignore* air resistance, in which case you'll just need to remember this *simple* and *really quite obvious formula*:

Kinetic energy GAINED = Potential Energy LOST

EXAMPLE: A mouldy tomato of mass 140g is dropped from a height of 1.7m. Calculate its speed as it hits the floor.

ANSWER: There are four key steps to this method — and you've gotta learn them:

Step 1) Find the PE lost: = mgh = 0.14 × 10 × 1.7 = **2.38J**. This must also be the KE gained.

Step 2) Equate the number of joules of KE gained to the KE formula with v in, "½mv²":
2.38 = ½mv²

Step 3) Stick the numbers in: 2.38 = ½ × 0.14 × v² or 2.38 = 0.07 × v²
2.38 ÷ 0.07 = v² so v² = 34

Step 4) Square root: v = √34 = **5.83 m/s**

Easy peasy? Not really no, but if you practise learning the four steps you'll find it's not too bad.

Revise falling objects — just don't lose your grip...

This is it. This is the zenith of GCSE Physics. This is the nearest it gets to *real* Physics (A-level). Look at that terrifying square root sign for a start — and a four step method. Scary stuff.

SEG SYLLABUS — SECTION FIVE — ENERGY RESOURCES & ENERGY TRANSFER

Revision Summary for Section Five

There are three distinct parts to Section Five. First there's power, work done, efficiency, etc., involving a lot of formulae and calculations. Then there's heat transfer, which is trickier to fully get to grips with than most people realise — and finally there's the stuff on generating power, which is basically easy but there are lots of drivelly details to learn. Make sure you realise the different approach needed for each bit and focus your planet-sized brain accordingly.

1) List the four non-renewable sources of energy and say why they are non-renewable.
2) List seven kinds of renewable energy.
3) Draw three energy chains that start with the Sun as the source of energy.
4) Where does the Sun's energy come from? How does this energy reach Earth?
5) Which kind of resources do we get most of our energy from? Sketch a typical power station.
6) Give full details of how we can use wind power, including the advantages and disadvantages.
7) Describe how solar panels work. What are their pros and cons?
8) What's pumped storage all about? What problem does it solve?
9) Sketch a wave generator and explain the pros and cons of this as a source of energy.
10) Explain how tidal power can be harnessed. What are the pros and cons of this method?
11) List ten different types of energy, and give twelve different examples of energy transfers.
12) What causes heat to flow from one place to another? What do molecules do as they heat up?
13) Explain what evaporation is. Write down the four factors that increase its rate.
14) Give a strict definition of conduction of heat and say which materials are good conductors.
15) What causes natural convection currents? Describe how they produce ocean currents.
16) List five properties of heat radiation. Which kind of objects emit and absorb heat radiation?
17) Which surfaces absorb heat radiation best? Which surfaces emit it best?
18) Describe two experiments to demonstrate the effect of different surfaces on radiant heat.
19) Explain briefly the difference between conduction, convection and radiation.
20) Describe insulation measures that reduce a) conduction   b) convection   c) radiation.
21) Name some materials that are good insulators and describe uses for them in the home.
22) List the seven main ways to reduce energy losses from houses.
23) Which types of heat transfer are insulated against in: a) double glazing; b) draught-proofing.
24) Draw a fully labelled diagram of a vacuum flask, and explain exactly what each bit is for.
25) Sketch the basic energy flow diagram for a typical "useful device".
26) What forms do the wasted energy always take?
27) What's the formula for efficiency?
28) Is efficiency really easy or really complicated? Give three worked examples on efficiency.
29) List seven environmental hazards with non-renewables and four ways that we can use less.
30) Why do we need to reduce our carbon dioxide emissions?
31) List the broad advantages and disadvantages of using renewable and non-renewable sources of energy. What does it mean when a question says "Discuss..."?
32) What's the connection between "work done" and "energy transferred"?
33) What's the formula for work done? A crazy dog drags a big branch 12m over the next-door neighbour's front lawn, pulling with a force of 535N. How much energy is transferred?
34) What's the formula for power? What are the units of power?
35) An electric motor uses 540kJ of electrical energy in 4½ minutes. What is its power consumption? If it has an efficiency of 85%, what's its power output?
36) Write down the formulae for KE and PE. Find the KE of a 78kg sheep moving at 23m/s.
37) Calculate the power output of a 78kg sheep that runs up a 20m high staircase in 16.5s.
38) Calculate the speed of a 78kg sheep as it hits the floor from a height of 20m.
39) If the sheep bounces back up to a height of 18m calculate the % loss of KE at the bounce.

SECTION FIVE — ENERGY RESOURCES & ENERGY TRANSFER   SEG SYLLABUS

RADIOACTIVITY

Atomic Structure

Characteristics and Detection

See the Chemistry Book for a few more details on this.

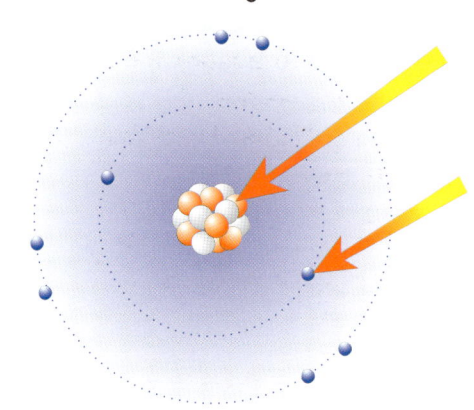

The NUCLEUS contains protons and neutrons. Most of the MASS of the atom is contained in the nucleus, but it takes up virtually no space — it's tiny.

The ELECTRONS fly around the outside. They're negatively charged and really really small. They occupy a lot of space and this gives the atom its overall size, even though it's mostly empty space. The number of electrons is equal to the number of protons. This means that the whole atom has no overall charge.

Make sure you learn this table:

PARTICLE	MASS	CHARGE
Proton	1	+1
Neutron	1	0
Electron	1/1,840	−1

THE MASS NUMBER
— Total of Protons and Neutrons
(Also known as the nucleon number)

THE ATOMIC NUMBER
— Number of Protons

$^{7}_{3}Li$

Isotopes Are Different Forms of the Same Element

1) All atoms of a particular element have the same number of protons.
2) Isotopes are atoms with the SAME number of protons, but a DIFFERENT number of neutrons.
3) Hence they have the same proton number, but a different mass number.
4) Carbon-12 and carbon-14 are good examples:
5) All elements have different isotopes — but there's usually only one or two stable ones.
6) Radioisotopes are radioactive isotopes, which means that they decay into other elements and give out radiation. This is where all radioactivity comes from — unstable radioactive isotopes undergoing nuclear decay and spitting out high energy particles.

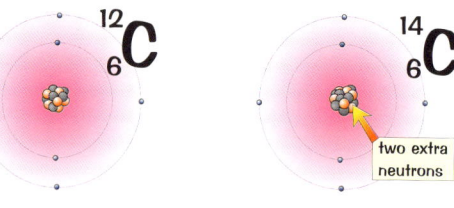

$^{12}_{6}C$ $^{14}_{6}C$ (two extra neutrons)

Rutherford's Scattering and the Demise of the Plum Pudding

1) In 1804 John Dalton said that matter was made up of tiny solid spheres, which he called atoms.
2) Later they discovered electrons could be removed from atoms. They then saw atoms as spheres of positive charge with tiny negative electrons stuck in them, like plums in a plum pudding.
3) Then Ernest Rutherford and his merry men tried firing alpha particles at a thin gold foil. Most of them just went straight through, but the odd one came straight back at them, which was frankly a bit of a shocker for Ernie and his pals. Being pretty clued up guys though, they realised this meant that most of the mass of the atom was concentrated at the centre in a tiny nucleus with a positive charge. This means that most of an atom is just made up of empty space, which is also a bit of a shocker when you think about it.

Plum pudding theory — by 1911 they'd had their fill of it...

Yeah, that's right — atoms are mostly empty space. When you think about it, those electrons are amazing little jokers really. They have almost no mass, no size, and a tiny little −ve charge. In the end it's only their frantic whizzing about that makes atoms what they are. It's outrageous.

SEG Syllabus   SECTION SIX — RADIOACTIVITY

Types of Radiation

Characteristics and Detection

Alpha (α), Beta (β) and Gamma (γ) Radiation

Alpha, beta and gamma radiation differ in the amount of material it takes to absorb them — see below. Don't get _mixed up_ between _nuclear_ radiation, which is _dangerous_ — and _electromagnetic_ radiation, which _generally isn't_. [Though if you're doing Higher Level don't forget that gamma radiation is a type of electromagnetic radiation — see P. 80].
A substance that gives out radiation all the time is called _radioactive_.

Radioactivity Is a Totally Random Process

Unstable nuclei will _decay_ and in the process _give out radiation_. This process is entirely _random_. This means that if you have 1,000 unstable nuclei, you can't say when _any one of them_ is going to decay, and neither can you do anything at all _to make a decay happen_.
Each nucleus will just decay quite _spontaneously_ in its _own good time_.
It's completely unaffected by _physical_ conditions like _temperature_, or by any sort of _chemical bonding_, etc.
When the nucleus _does_ decay it will _spit out_ one or more of the three types of radiation, _alpha_, _beta_ or _gamma_, and in the process the _nucleus_ will often _change_ into a _new element_.

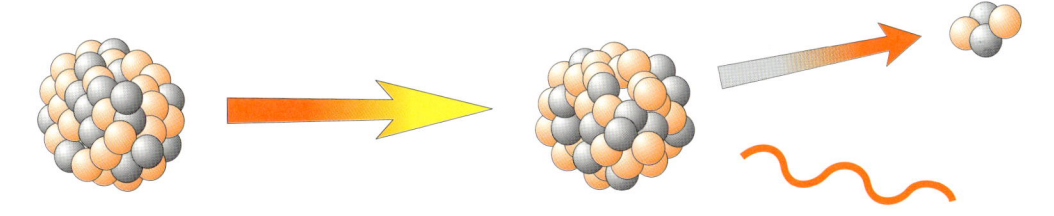

Remember What Blocks Each Type of Radiation...

As radiation _passes through_ materials some of the radiation is _absorbed_. The greater the _thickness_ of material, the _more absorption_.

They really like this for Exam questions, so make sure _you know_ what it takes to _block_ each of the _three_:

ALPHA particles are blocked by _paper_.
BETA particles are blocked by thin _aluminium_.
GAMMA rays are blocked by _thick lead_.

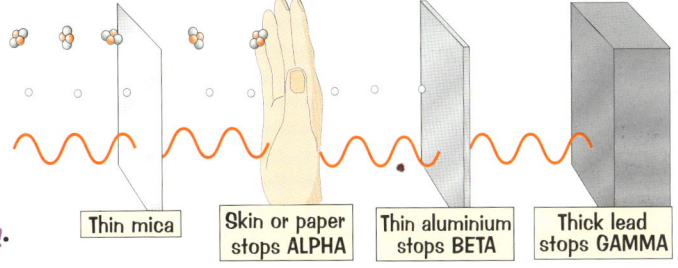

Thin mica | Skin or paper stops ALPHA | Thin aluminium stops BETA | Thick lead stops GAMMA

Of course anything _equivalent_ will also block them, e.g. _skin_ will stop _alpha_, but _not_ the others; a thin sheet of _any metal_ will stop _beta_; and _very thick concrete_ will stop _gamma_ just like lead does.

Learn the three types of radiation — it's easy as abc...

Alpha, beta and gamma. You do realise those are just the first three letters of the Greek alphabet don't you: α, β, γ — just like a, b, c. They might sound like complex names to you but they were just easy labels at the time. Anyway, _learn all the facts_ about them — and _scribble_.

SECTION SIX — RADIOACTIVITY
SEG SYLLABUS

Types of Radiation

Characteristics and Detection

Nuclear Radiation: Alpha, Beta and Gamma

You need to remember *three things* about *each type of radiation*:
1) What they actually *are*.
2) How well they *penetrate* materials.
3) How strongly they *ionise* that material (i.e. bash into atoms and *knock electrons off*).
   There's a pattern: The *further* the radiation can *penetrate* before hitting an atom and getting stopped, the *less damage* it will do along the way, and so the *less ionising* it is.

Alpha Particles Are Helium Nuclei

1) They are relatively *big* and *heavy* and *slow moving*.
2) They therefore *don't* penetrate into materials, but are *stopped quickly*.
3) Because of their size they are *strongly* ionising, which just means they *bash into* a lot of atoms and *knock electrons off* them before they slow down, which creates lots of ions — hence the term *"ionising"*.
4) An α-*particle* is simply a *helium nucleus* with a mass of 4 and a charge of +2, made up of 2 protons and 2 neutrons ($^4_2$He).

A typical *alpha emission*:

$^{226}_{88}$Ra (Unstable isotope) → $^{222}_{86}$Rn (New isotope) + $^4_2$He (Alpha particle)

Beta Particles Are Electrons

1) These are *in between* alpha and gamma in terms of their *properties*.
2) They move *quite* fast and they are *quite* small (they're electrons).
3) They *penetrate moderately* before colliding and are *moderately ionising* too.
4) For every β *particle* emitted, a *neutron* turns to a *proton* in the nucleus.
5) A β *particle* is simply an *electron*, with virtually no mass and a charge of -1 ($^{\ 0}_{-1}$e). *Every time* a beta particle is emitted from the nucleus, a *neutron* in the nucleus is *converted* to a *proton*.

A typical *beta emission*:

$^{14}_{6}$C (Unstable isotope) → $^{14}_{7}$N (New isotope) + $^{\ 0}_{-1}$e (Beta particle)

Gamma Rays Are Very Short Wavelength EM Waves

1) They are the *opposite* of alpha particles in a way.
2) They *penetrate a long way* into materials without being stopped.
3) This means they are *weakly* ionising because they tend to *pass through* rather than colliding with atoms. Eventually they *hit something* and do *damage*.
4) A γ-*ray* is an *electromagnetic wave* with no mass or charge, but with a *very high frequency*.
5) After an *alpha or beta emission* the nucleus sometimes has *extra energy to get rid of*. It does this by emitting a *gamma ray*. Gamma emission *never changes* the *proton or mass numbers* of the nucleus.

A typical combined α *and* γ *emission*:

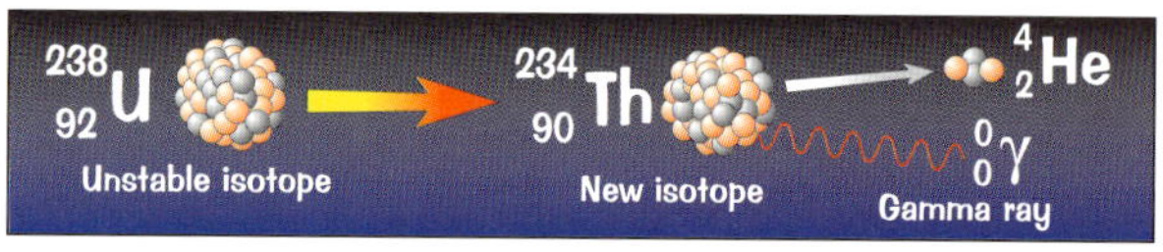

$^{238}_{92}$U (Unstable isotope) → $^{234}_{90}$Th (New isotope) + $^4_2$He + $^0_0\gamma$ (Gamma ray)

Alpha give the odd mistake — just don't beta lazy to learn it...

That's right. Lots more info. on those three lovely types of radiation: alpha particles, beta particles and gamma rays. *Learn all the gory details*, then cover the page and jot them down in three little mini-essays. It's a piece of plum pudding, surely it is.

SEG Syllabus

SECTION SIX — RADIOACTIVITY

Background Radiation

Characteristics and Detection

Background Radiation Comes from Many Sources

Background radiation comes from:

1) Radioactivity of naturally occurring substances <u>all around us</u> — in the <u>air</u>, in <u>food</u>, in <u>building materials</u>, and in the <u>rocks</u> under our feet.

2) Radiation from <u>space</u>, which is known as <u>cosmic rays</u>. These come mostly from the <u>Sun</u>.

3) Radiation due to <u>human activity</u>, e.g. <u>fallout</u> from <u>nuclear explosions</u> or <u>dumped nuclear waste</u>. This represents a <u>tiny</u> proportion of the total background radiation.

Where the radiation *ENTERING OUR BODIES* typically comes from:

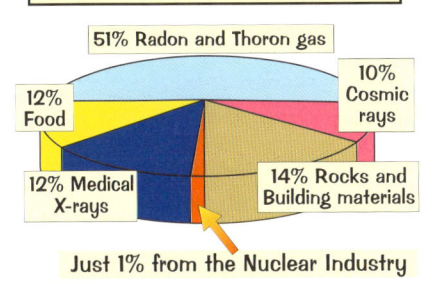

- 51% Radon and Thoron gas
- 10% Cosmic rays
- 12% Food
- 14% Rocks and Building materials
- 12% Medical X-rays
- Just 1% from the Nuclear Industry

Detecting Radiation — the Geiger-Müller Tube and Counter

1) This is the most <u>familiar type</u> of <u>radiation detector</u>. You see them on TV documentaries going <u>click-click-clickety-click</u>, whilst the grim-faced reporter delivers his sombre message of impending doom and the terrible state of the planet.

2) This is also the type used for <u>experiments in the lab</u>, as the counter allows you to record the number of <u>counts per minute</u>.

3) When an <u>alpha</u>, <u>beta</u> or <u>gamma</u> enters the <u>G-M tube</u>, it causes a small pulse of electricity which is sent to the electronic <u>counter</u>. It can also be amplified and fed to a loudspeaker to give that characteristic <u>clicking sound</u>.

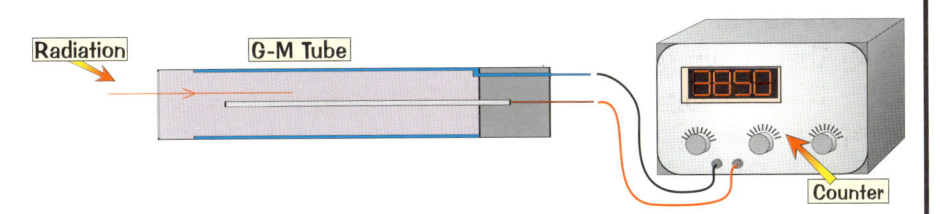

If you want to find the <u>count rate</u> from a <u>specific source</u>, you must always measure the <u>background count</u> first, (i.e. take the reading with <u>no source</u> present) and then <u>subtract</u> that value from <u>each reading</u> taken using the source. This is <u>especially important</u> if you are plotting the values on a <u>graph</u> to find the <u>half-life</u>.

Photographic Film Also Detects Radiation

1) Radiation was first <u>discovered by accident</u> when <u>Henri Becquerel</u> left some <u>uranium</u> on some <u>photographic plates</u>, which became "<u>fogged</u>" by it.

2) These days <u>photographic film</u> is a useful way of detecting radiation.

3) Workers in the <u>nuclear industry</u> or those using <u>X-ray equipment</u> such as <u>dentists</u> and <u>radiographers</u> wear <u>little blue badges</u> that have a bit of <u>photographic film</u> in them.

4) The film is checked <u>every now and then</u> to see if it's got fogged <u>too quickly</u>, which would mean that the person was getting <u>too great an exposure</u> to radiation.

Background radiation — it's no good burying your head in the sand...

Make sure you remember those two ways of measuring radiation: G-M tube and photographic film. And don't forget that you need a counter as well as the G-M tube — it's not much cop without one. This page is ideal for the good old mini-essay method I reckon, just to make sure you've taken all the important points on board. So <u>learn and scribble</u>.

SECTION SIX — RADIOACTIVITY

Half-life

Characteristics and Detection

The Radioactivity of a Sample Always Decreases over Time

1) This is *pretty obvious* when you think about it. Each time a *decay* happens and an alpha, beta or gamma is given out, it means one more *radioactive* nucleus has *disappeared*.

2) Obviously, as the *unstable nuclei* all steadily disappear, the *activity* as a whole will also *decrease*. So the *older* a sample becomes, the *less* radiation it will emit.

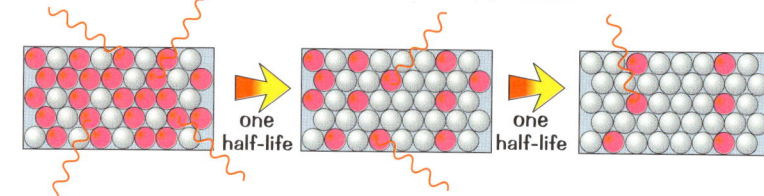

3) *How quickly* the activity *drops off* varies a lot from one radioisotope to another. For *some* it can take *just a few hours* before nearly all the unstable nuclei have *decayed*, whilst others can last for *millions of years*.

4) The problem with trying to *measure* this is that the activity *never reaches ZERO*, which is why we have to use the idea of *HALF-LIFE* to measure how quickly the activity *drops off*.

5) Learn this *important definition* of *half-life*:

HALF-LIFE is the TIME TAKEN for THE NUMBER OF PARENT atoms in a sample to HALVE.

(The number of parent atoms is the number of atoms in the original radioactive source)

Another definition of half-life is: "The time taken for the activity (or count rate) of the original substance to fall to half it's original level". Use either.

6) A *short half-life* means the activity falls *quickly*, because *lots* of the nuclei decay *quickly*.

7) A *long half-life* means the activity falls *more slowly* because *most* of the nuclei don't decay for a *long time* — they just sit there, *unstable*, but kind of *biding their time*.

Measuring the Half-Life of a Sample Using a Graph

1) *Several readings* are taken of *count rate* and the results can then be *plotted* as a *graph*, which will *always* be shaped like the one below.

2) The *half-life* is found from the graph, by finding the *time interval* on the *bottom axis* corresponding to a *halving* of the *activity* on the *vertical axis*. Easy peasy really.

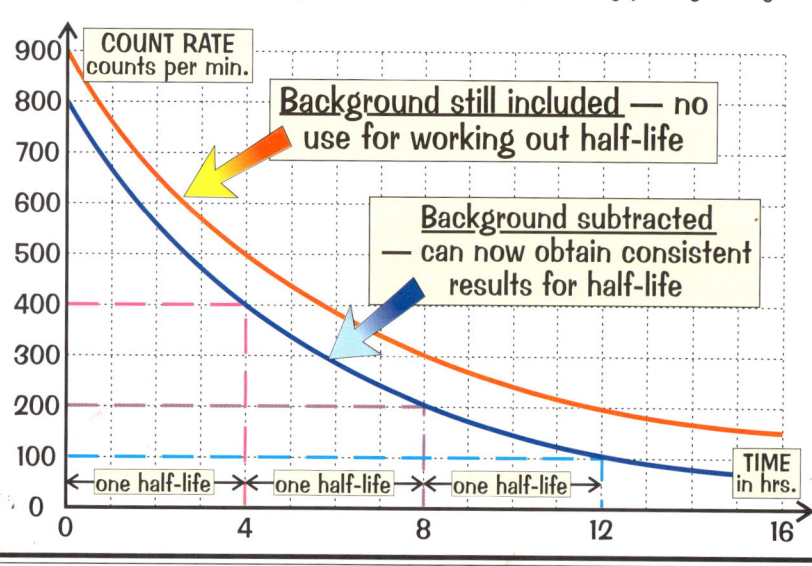

One trick you really do need to know about is the business of the *background radiation*, which also adds to the count and gives *false readings*. You have to measure the background count *first* and then *subtract it* from *every* reading you get, before plotting the results on the *graph*. Realistically, the only *difficult bit* is actually *remembering* about that for your *Exam*, should they ask you about it. They could also test that idea in a *calculation question*, like those on the next page.

Definition of half-life — a freshly woken teenager...

People can get really confused by the idea of half-life. Remember — a radioactive sample will never completely decay away because the amount left just keeps halving. So the only way to measure how long it "lasts", is to time how long it takes to drop by half. That's all it is. Peasy

Half-life Calculations

Characteristics and Detection

The basic idea of half-life is maybe a little confusing, but Exam calculations are *pretty straightforward*, so long as you do them slowly, **STEP BY STEP**, like this one:

A VERY SIMPLE EXAMPLE: The activity of a radioisotope is 640cpm (counts per minute). Two hours later it has fallen to 40 counts per minute. Find the half-life of the sample.

ANSWER: You must go through it in *SHORT SIMPLE STEPS* like this:

INITIAL count:		after ONE half-life:		after TWO half-lives:		after THREE half-lives:		after FOUR half-lives:
640	(÷2)→	320	(÷2)→	160	(÷2)→	80	(÷2)→	40

Notice the careful *step-by-step method*, which tells us that it takes *four half-lives* for the activity to fall from 640 to 40. Hence *two hours* represents four half-lives so *the half-life is 30 minutes*.

Carbon-14 Calculations — or Radiocarbon Dating

Carbon-14 makes up about 1/10,000,000 (one *ten-millionth*) of the carbon in the *air*. This level stays fairly *constant* in the *atmosphere*. The same proportion of C-14 is also found in *living things*. However, when they *die*, the C-14 is trapped *inside* the wood or wool or whatever, and it gradually *decays* with a *half-life* of *5,600 years*. By simply measuring the *proportion* of C-14 found in some old *axe handle*, *burial shroud*, etc., you can easily calculate *how long ago* the item was living material.

EXAMPLE: An axe handle was found to contain 1 part in 40,000,000 carbon-14. Calculate the age of the axe.

ANSWER: The C-14 was originally *1 part in 10,000,000*. After *one half-life* it would be down to *1 part in 20,000,000*. After *two half-lives* it would be down to *1 part in 40,000,000*. Hence the axe handle is *two C-14 half-lives* old, i.e. 2 × 5,600 = *11,200 YEARS OLD*.

Note the same old *step-wise method*, going down one half-life at a time.

Relative Proportions Calculations — Easy, So Long as You Learn It

Uranium isotopes have a *very long* half-life and decay via a *series* of short-lived particles to produce *stable isotopes* of lead. The *relative proportions* of uranium and lead isotopes in a sample of *igneous* rock can therefore be used to *date* the rock, using the *known half-life* of the uranium. It's as simple as this:

INITIALLY:	*After one half-life:*	*After two half-lives:*	*After three half-lives:*
100% uranium	50% uranium	25% uranium	12.5% uranium
0% lead	50% lead	75% lead	87.5% lead

Ratio of uranium to lead: (half-life of uranium-238 = 4.5 billion years)

Initially:	After *one half-life:*	After *two half-lives:*	After *three half-lives:*
1:0	1:1	1:3	1:7

Similarly, the proportions of *potassium-40* and its stable decay product *argon-40* can also be used to *date igneous rocks*, so long as the *argon gas* hasn't been able to *escape*. The *relative proportions* will be exactly the *same* as for the uranium and lead example above. *Learn these ratios*:

Initially:	*After one half-life:*	*After two half-lives:*	*After three half-lives:*
100% : 0%	50% : 50%	25% : 75%	12.5% : 87.5%
1:0	1:1	1:3	1:7

Learn about half-life — and get things in proportion...

These half-life calculations are really pretty simple. Try these:
1) An isotope has a half-life of 12 mins. How long will it take to drop from 840cpm to 210cpm?
2) A sample of rock contains uranium-238 and lead in the ratio 75:525. How old is the rock?

SECTION SIX — RADIOACTIVITY *SEG SYLLABUS*

Radiation and the Body

Effects and Uses

Radiation Harms Living Cells

1) *Alpha*, *beta* and *gamma* radiation will cheerfully enter living cells and *collide* with molecules.
2) These collisions cause *ionisation*, which *damages* or *destroys* the molecules.
3) *Lower* doses tend to cause *minor* damage without *killing* the cell.
4) This can give rise to *mutant* cells, which divide *uncontrollably*. This is *cancer*.
5) *Higher* doses tend to *kill cells* completely, which causes *radiation sickness* if a lot of your body cells *all get blatted at once*.
6) The *extent* of the harmful effects depends on *two things*:
    a) How much *exposure* you have to the radiation.
    b) The *energy* and *penetration* of the radiation emitted, since some types are *more hazardous* than others, of course.

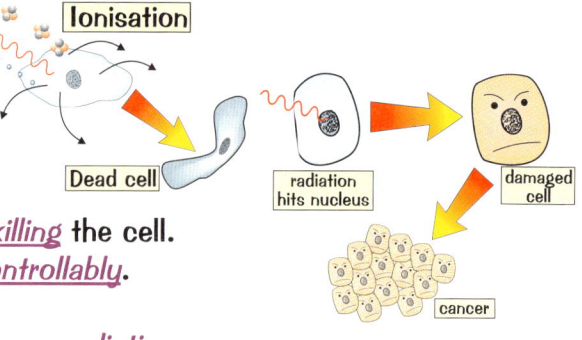

Outside the Body, β and γ Sources Are the Most Dangerous

This is because *beta and gamma* can get *inside* to the delicate *organs*, whereas alpha is much less dangerous because it *can't penetrate* the skin.

Inside the Body, an α Source Is the Most Dangerous

Inside the body alpha sources do all their damage in a *very localised area*. Beta and gamma sources on the other hand are *less dangerous* inside the body because they mostly *pass straight out* without doing much damage.

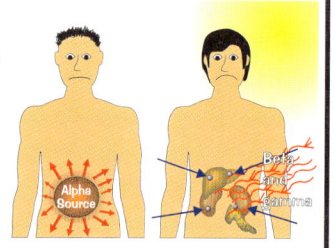

Radiation Can Also Be Useful in Medicine...

1) Radiotherapy — the Treatment of Cancer Using γ-Rays

1) Since high doses of gamma rays will *kill all living cells*, they can be used to *treat cancers*.
2) The gamma rays have to be *directed carefully* and at just the right *dosage*, so as to kill the *cancer cells* without damaging too many *normal cells*.

2) Tracers in Medicine — Always Short Half-Life γ-Emitters

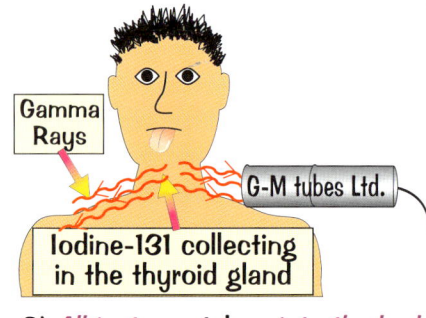

1) Certain *radioactive isotopes* can be *injected* into people (or they can just *swallow* them) and their progress *around the body* can be followed with a *detector*. A computer is used to convert the reading to a *TV display*, showing where the *strongest* reading is coming from. A well-known example is the use of *iodine-131*, which is absorbed by the *thyroid gland*, just like normal iodine-127. The iodine-131 gives out *radiation* that can be *detected* to indicate whether or not the thyroid gland is *taking in the iodine* as it should.
2) *All isotopes* taken *into the body* must be *GAMMA sources* (never alpha or beta), so that the radiation *passes out* of the body. They must also have a *short* half-life of just *a few hours*, so that the radioactivity inside the patient *quickly* disappears.

Radiation sickness — well yes, it does all get a bit tedious...

Quite a few picky details here. It's easy to kid yourself that you don't really need to know all this stuff. Well take it from me, you *do* need to know it all and there's only one sure-fire way to find out whether you do or not. *Mini-essays* please, with all the picky details in. Enjoy.

SEG Syllabus

SECTION SIX — RADIOACTIVITY

Uses of Radioactive Materials

Effects and Uses

1) Tracers in Industry — for Finding Leaks

This is _much the same technique_ as the medical tracers. 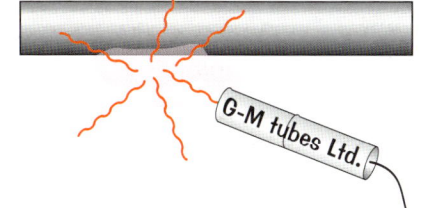
1) Radioisotopes can be used to detect _leaks_ in pipes.
2) You just _squirt it in_, and then use a detector _outside_ the pipe to find areas of _extra high_ radioactivity, which indicates that stuff is _leaking out_. This is real useful for _underground_ pipes, to save you digging up half the road trying to find the leak.
3) The isotope used _must_ be a _gamma emitter_, so that the radiation can be _detected_ even through _metal or earth_, which may be _surrounding_ the pipe. Alpha and beta rays wouldn't be much use because they are easily _blocked_ by any surrounding material.
4) It should also have a _short half-life_, so as not to cause a _hazard_ if it collects somewhere.

2) Thickness Control in Industry and Manufacturing

This is a classic application and is _pretty popular in Exams_. It's really very simple.
1) You have a _radioactive source_ and you direct it _through_ the stuff being made — usually a continuous sheet of _paper_ or _cardboard_ or _metal_, etc.

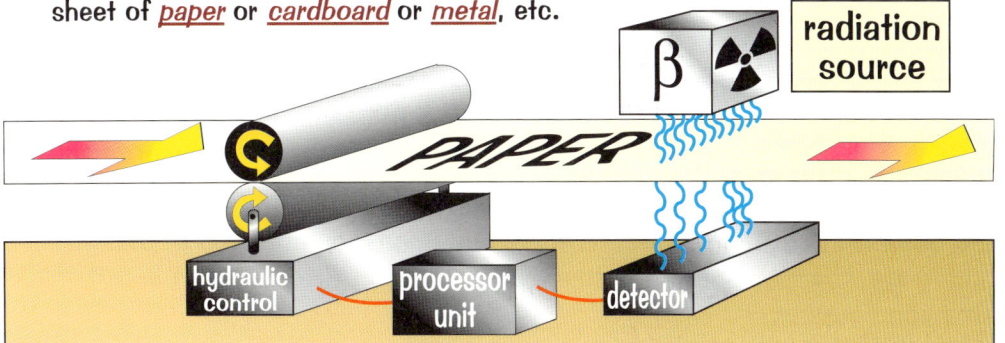

2) The _detector_ is on the _other side_ and is connected to a _control unit_.

3) When the amount of radiation detected _goes down_, it means the stuff is coming out _too thick_, and so the control unit _pinches the rollers up_ a bit to make it _thinner_ again.
4) If the reading _goes up_, it means it's _too thin_, so the control unit _opens the rollers out_ a bit.

It's all clever stuff, but the most _important_ thing, as usual, is the _choice of isotope_:

1) First and foremost it must have a nice _long half-life_ (of several _years_ at least!), otherwise the strength would gradually _decline_ and the silly control unit would keep _pinching up_ the rollers trying to _compensate_.
2) Secondly, the source must be a _BETA source_ for _paper and cardboard_, or a _GAMMA source_ for _metal sheets_. This is because the stuff being made must **PARTLY** block the radiation.
If it _all_ goes through, (or _none_ of it does), then the reading _won't change_ at all as the thickness changes. Alpha particles are no use for this since they would _all be stopped_.

Radioactive Materials Can Be a Bit of a Nightmare

These _handy uses_ of radiation are all _well and good_, but don't forget that the _increased use_ of radioactive materials can lead to _social_, _economic_ and _environmental_ problems. These include:
1) The risk of _leaks_ of radioactive material, which can be _dangerous_ and _very expensive_ to clean up.
2) The _pollution_ and other _environmental problems_ caused by the _mining_ of the radioactive isotopes.
3) The _expense_ of and _pollution_ caused by _disposal_ of the radioactive materials after they've been used.
4) The _dangers_ to _workers_ who use the radioactive materials from day to day.

Will any of that be in your Exam? — isotope so...

First _learn_ the headings till you can write them down _from memory_. Then start _learning_ all the details that go with each one of them. As usual, the best way to check what you know is to do a _mini-essay_ for each section. Then check back and see what details you _missed_. Nicely.

SECTION SIX — RADIOACTIVITY   SEG SYLLABUS

Revision Summary for Section Six

It's an outrage — just so much stuff you've gotta learn — it's all work, work, work, no time to rest, no time to play. But then that's the grim cruel reality of life in 1990s Britain — just drudgery, hard work and untold weariness... "And then he woke up and it had all been a dream..." Yeah, maybe life's not so bad after all — even for hard-done-to teenagers. Just a few jolly bits and bobs to learn in warm, cosy, comfortable civilisation. Practise these questions over and over again till you can answer them all effortlessly. Smile and enjoy. ☺

1) Sketch an atom. Give three details about the nucleus and the electrons.
2) Draw up a wee table detailing the mass and charge of the three basic subatomic particles.
3) Explain what the mass number and proton number of an atom represent.
4) Write down the number of electrons, protons and neutrons there are in an atom of $^{226}_{88}Ra$, and say what its overall charge would be.
5) Explain what isotopes are. Give an example. Are most isotopes stable or unstable?
6) What was the Plum Pudding model? Who put paid to that crazy old idea?
7) Describe Rutherford's scattering experiment with a diagram, and say what happened.
8) What was the inevitable conclusion to be drawn from this experiment?
9) What is the main difference between EM radiation and nuclear radiation?
10) What are the three types of radiation, and how do they compare in penetrating power and ionising power?
11) List several things that will block each of the three types.
12) Will anything cause a nucleus to undergo radioactive decay? What about nuclear fission?
12) Describe in detail the nature and properties of the three types of radiation: α, β, and γ.
14) Sketch a fairly accurate pie chart to show the how much radiation the average person absorbs from the six main sources.
15) List three places where the level of background radiation is increased, and explain why it is.
16) Name two ways to detect radiation, and explain how the equipment is used in each case.
17) Sketch a diagram to show how the activity of a sample keeps halving.
18) Give a proper definition of half-life. How long and how short can half-lives be?
19) Sketch a typical graph of activity against time. Show how the half-life can be found.
20) What's the single most important thing to remember when doing half-life calculations?
21) An old bit of cloth was found to have 1 atom of C-14 to 80,000,000 atoms of C-12. Using the information on P. 83, calculate the age of the bit of cloth.
22) A rock contains uranium-238 atoms and stable lead atoms in the ratio 1:3. If the half-life of uranium-238 is 4.5×10^9 years, how old is the rock?
23) Exactly what kind of damage does radiation do inside body cells?
24) What damage do low doses cause? What effects do higher doses have?
25) Which kinds of sources are most dangerous   a) inside the body   b) outside the body?
26) Describe a situation where the killing of living cells by gamma rays can be helpful.
27) Describe in detail how radioactive isotopes are used in each of the following:
   a) tracers in medicine   b) tracers in industry   c) thickness control.
28) Briefly describe some social, economic and environmental problems due to uses of radioactive materials.

Answers   **P.20** **Revn Sumy** **38) a)** 0.125A   **b)** 240C   **c)** 321W   **d)** 14Ω   **e)** 240kJ
P.34 **Revn Sumy** **2)** 0.09m/s, 137m   **7)** 3.5m/s²   **11)** 7.5m/s²   **12)** 5.7kg   **35)** 3,120cm³   **P.36** **1)** 330m/s
2) 200kHz   **P.48** **1)** 198m   **2)** 490m   **P.50** **Revn Sumy** **8) a)** 500,000 Hz   **b)** 0.35m   **c)** 4,600,000 Hz   **d)** 0.04m/s
e) 150s   **9)** 150m/s   **10)** 200 kHz   **39)** 1980m   **40)** 0.86s   **P.59** **Revn Sumy** **29)** Real strange, The Bentley Turbo
P.77 **Revn Sumy** **33)** 6,420J   **35)** 2,000W, 1,700W   **36)** 20,631J   **37)** 945W   **38)** 20m/s   **39)** 10%
P.83 **1)** 24mins   **2)** 13.5 billion years   **P.86** **Revn Sumy** **21)** 16,800 yrs   **22)** 9×10^9 yrs

Index

A
absorbed 42, 43, 62
absorbing 68
AC 15, 16, 17
acceleration 23, 27, 28, 76
ace practice 20
acetate rod 1
air resistance 22, 28, 76
alpha particles/emission 79, 80, 82, 84
alternating current. 15, 16, 17
ammeter 4
amplitude 35, 45
amps 4
angle of incidence 37, 38
aquaplaning 26
arctic circle 54
areas of pistons 32
argon-40 83
atmospheres 33
atomic structure 78
attraction 1, 11, 57

B
background radiation 81, 82
balanced forces 23
bar magnet 11
bats, ultrasound 47
batteries 9, 64
battery 4
bell jar experiment 45
bending 29
beta particles/emission 79, 80, 82, 84, 85
Big Bang theory 57
big rotating ball 54
binoculars 40
boiler 17
boiler, fancy 61
brakes 26
braking distance 26
brass 4
broken bones 44
broken wrists 13
burglar detectors 5
buzz 17

C
cables 18
cancer 44, 84
car brakes 32
cavity wall insulation 69, 70
Celsius temperature 65
cells 6, 10
charges 1, 10
chemical energy 64
Christmas fairy lights 7
circuits 6, 8, 10
circuit breaker 18
circular barrier/ripples 37
clothes and blankets 69
clothing crackles 2
coal 60, 61

coil of wire 12, 15
colours 39
comets 52
communications 40, 42
compass 11
components 4, 10
compressing 29
compressions 35
conduction, heat 65, 66, 70
conservation 73
constellations 52
convection currents 67
convection, heat 65, 67, 69, 70
cooking foil 69
cooking food 43
cooling fins 69
Copernicus 52
core 12, 49
cosmic rays 81
cost = units × price 19
coulomb 10
cricket, speed of sound 48
critical angle 39, 40
CRO displays 15, 35, 46
current, electrical 4, 6, 8, 10, 12, 13, 17, 18
current-carrying wire 11
curtains 70

D
Dalton, John 78
damaging surfaces 31
dangerous 42, 43, 44, 73, 84
days and seasons 54
DC supply 13, 15
decay, radioactive 79, 82
deceleration 24, 26
definitely uncool 37
density 31, 44, 45, 49, 67
depth, pressure 31
details swirling around 25
diffraction 41, 42
diode 4, 5
dippy little engines 73
direct current 13, 15
dispersion 39
dissipated as heat 65, 76
distance-time graphs 21
doom and gloom 73
Doppler effect 57
dosage of radiation 44
double glazing 70
double insulation 18
drag 22, 24, 28
draught-proofing 70
drawing pins 31
driving force 3
dust 58
dynamo 14, 15

E
Earth 51, 52, 58
earth wire 18
earthing and fuses 18
earthing straps, anti-static 2
earthquakes 49

Earth's atmosphere 43, 55
Earth's magnetic field 11
eccentric orbits 53
echo questions 48
echoes 45
eddy currents 16
elastic 64
elastic limit 30
elastic potential energy 64, 75
electric bell 12
electric heaters 71
electric motor 13
electrical charge/circuits 10
electrical energy 64
electrical oscillations 47
electrical power 19
electrical pressure 3
electrical signals 46
electricity 17
electricity meter 19
electromagnetic induction 16
electromagnetic waves/ radiation/spectrum 42, 51, 68, 79
electrons 1, 66, 78
elements 78
EM waves 60
EM waves/radiation 36, 51, 80
endoscope 44
endoscopes 40
energy dissipation 71
energy flow diagram 71
energy input/output 72
energy, of waves 10, 35, 45, 66, 74, 75
energy transfer 64, 71, 72
equilibrium 29
evaporation 65
exposure, radiation 44, 81, 84
extension, Hooke's law 30

F
factor of two, echoes 48
fair old effort 69
falling objects 76
feels hotter or colder 66
fibre glass wool 70
filament lamp 4
Fleming's left hand rule 13
fluorescent tubes 44
food 64, 74, 81
force 13
force, area, pressure 31
force diagrams 22, 23, 24, 28
force of attraction 2, 27, 52
force of gravity 58
formula triangle 21
fossil fuels 60, 73
foundations, pressure 31
free electrons, in metals 66
free-fallers, terminal velocity 28
frequency, of waves 35, 36, 41, 43, 46, 47, 57

friction 1, 22, 74
fuel-filling nightmare 2, 18, 64
funny old stuff 31
fuse ratings 19

G
galaxies 56, 57
gamma sources/emission 44, 79, 80, 82, 84, 85
gas syringe experiments 33
generating power 62
generators 15, 17
geographic poles 11
glass block demo 38
gradient 4, 21
grain shoots, static 2
graph, for half-life 82
gravitational attraction 60
gravitational potential energy 64
gravity 2, 27, 28, 52, 53, 57, 58, 63
greenhouse effect 73
grim up North 26
gripping facts 56

H
hairdrier 10
half-life 82, 83, 85
half-life calculations 83
harmful/harmless 42, 43, 44
hazards 26, 63
hearing 47
heat radiation 43, 68, 69
heat transfer 65, 70
heat when a current flows 10
heat will flow 65
heat/heat energy 51, 58, 64, 65, 67, 71
heating 42
height 75
helium nuclei 80
hideously easy 27
hideously important 4
hideously simple 72
high doses 44
higher doses 84
Hooke's law 30
household electrics 8
how dopey you are 26
hydraulics, jacks, brakes 32

I
ice skates, pressure 31
igneous rock 83
image, in plane mirror 37
immersion heater 10
incidence, angle of 37, 38
induced voltage 14, 15
induction, electromagnetic 17
inelastic behaviour 29
inescapable conclusion 57
infrared (or IR) 39, 43, 64, 68

input energy 71
instant regurgitation 34
insulating materials 1
insulators 66, 69
inverse proportion 33
iodine-131 84
ionisation 80, 84
iron core 12, 13, 16
iron rocker 12
isotopes 78
it's shocking 18

J
jet aircraft 48
jolly questions 34
joules 19, 64, 74, 75
juicy marks 55, 67
Jupiter 51, 52

K
kHz (kilohertz) 36
kill cells, radiation 43, 84
kilowatt-hours 19
kinetic energy 26, 64, 65, 75

L
laminated iron core 16
law of reflection 37
LDR 5
light 35, 37, 41, 48
light bulb 10
light dependent resistor 5
light energy 64
lightning 2, 48
little joker 66, 78
live cricket 48
live wire 18
load 30
loft insulation 69, 70
longitudinal waves 35, 45, 49
losses, energy 71
lots of drivelly details 77
lots of jolly details 63
loud noise, amplitude 45
loudspeakers 64
low polar orbit satellites 55
lower doses 44, 84

M
magnetic field 12, 13, 14
Mars 51, 52
mass 27, 29, 52, 75
mass balance 27
mass number 78
master piston, hydraulics 32
matt black, surfaces 69
maximum speed 28
media, for waves 38, 39, 42, 45, 68
Mercury 51, 52
metals 66, 69
MHz (megahertz) 36
microwaves, ovens 43

Index

Milky Way galaxy 56
molten lava 49
moons 52, 53
most grisly 20
mostly empty space 56, 78
moths in mid-flight 47
motor, motor effect 13
mutant cells, cancer 84

N

narrow gap, diffraction 41
national grid 17
natural convection 67
natural gas 60
natural satellites 53
Neptune 51, 52
neutral wire 18
neutrons 78
Newton, Isaac 23
newton meter 27
newtons 22, 27
night-time electricity 62
non-metals 66, 69
non-renewables 60, 61, 73
normal, light rays 37, 38
northern hemisphere 54
nuclear decay 78
nuclear energy/fuel 60, 64
nuclear fusion 58
nuclear fusion reactions 60
nuclear radiation 79
nuclear waste 81
nucleus/nuclei 78, 82
numb and weary mind 31

O

ocean currents 67
oil 60, 61
optical fibres 40, 44
orbits 27, 51, 52
oscilloscope display 15, 35, 46
outrageous improbability 59
overhead cables 1

P

P-waves, seismic waves 49
parachute 28
parallel 4
parallel circuits 8
partly chewed mouse 34
pascal, Pa 32
P.D. 4, 6, 8
peak demand 62, 63
peculiar movement of the planets 52
penetration, radiation 80
periscopes 40
perspex 39
photographic film 81
pitch, sound waves 46
plane mirror 37
plane waves 37
planetary nebula 58
planets 51, 52, 53
plum pudding 78
Pluto 51, 52
pockets of air, insulation 69
pollution 61
polythene rod, static 1
potassium-40 83
potential difference 4, 6, 8
potential energy 75, 76
power 17, 74, 76
power loss 17
power stations 17, 61
power supply 6, 17
pressure 31, 32, 33
pressure in liquids 31, 32
pretty bad news 3
pretty tricky 14, 40
primary coil 16
prisms 39, 40
proportional 30
pros and cons 77
proton number 78
protons 78
protostar 58
pump 3
pylons and cables 17

R

radiant heat 64
radiation hazards 84
radiation, heat 42, 65, 70
radiation, nuclear 79, 82
radiation sickness 84
radio waves 41, 42
radiocarbon dating 83
radioactive nightmare 85
radioactivity, radioisotopes, etc. 78, 79, 82
radiographers, X-rays 44
radiotherapy 84
rainbows, dispersion 39
rarefactions, waves 35
reaction forces 22, 25
real horrors 51
rectangular glass block 38
red giant 58
red-shift 57
reflection 37, 42
refraction 38, 39, 49
relay 12
remote controls, for TV 43
renewables, fuels 60, 61, 73
repelling 1, 11
resistance 6, 8, 17
resistance, force 28
resistance is futile 4
resultant force 23
reverberation 45
ridiculous idea 23
ripple tank 37, 38, 41
ripples 35
robots in disguise 16
rock and ice 53
rubber bands 64
run upstairs, power 76
Rutherford's scattering 78

S

S-waves, seismic waves 49
safety features 18
satellite transmissions 43
satellites 52
Saturn 51, 52
scientific research 44
secondary coil, transformer 16
security marks 44
seismic waves 35, 49
seismographs 49
semiconductor diode 5
series 4
series circuits 6, 7
seriously easy 30
shallower water 38
sharp knives, pressure 31
shearing 29
shock, electrical 1
shock waves 35, 49
shocks 18
shroud, dating of 83
SI units 36
sideways vibrations 35
silvered finishes 69
skin cancer 44
skulking cat 22
skydiver 28
slave piston, hydraulics 32
slightly tricky formula 75
slinky spring 35
slip rings, generator 15
slippy roads 26
snow shoes 31
"soft" iron 12
soft iron core 13
soggy pea 34
solar energy 62
solar power 60
Solar System 51, 52, 55
solenoid 11, 12
sonar 47, 48
sound 36, 41, 45, 47, 48
sound energy 64
sound waves 35, 45, 47
southern hemisphere 54
Spanish Inquisition 52
spark 1, 2
speakers 46
spectrum 42
speed 21, 26, 36, 75, 76
speed of falling objects 76
speed of sound 48
spiddly little cars 73
spring balance 27
springs 64
stars 52, 58
starting pistol, sound 48
static charges 1, 2
static electricity 1, 2, 3
steady speed 23, 24, 28
steel, magnetically hard 11
step-down/step-up transformers 16
sterilisation 44
stilettos, pressure 31
stopping distances 26
stored energy 64
stretching 29
submarines, pressure 31
Sun 51, 56, 58, 60, 64, 68, 81
sunbeds, UV rays 44
supernova 58
surface colour/texture 68, 69
survival blankets, silvered 69
sweating 65
sweaty velcro 39

T

take a few butties 56
temperature detectors 5
tension 22, 29
testing components 4
the bill 19
the sheep bounces back 77
thermal energy 64
thermostats 5, 70
thickness control 85
thinking distance 26
thrust 22
thunder and lightning 48
thyroid gland 84
tidal energy 60
tidal power, energy 63
toss big boats around 35
total internal reflection 39, 40
tracers in medicine 84
tractor tyres, pressure 31
transformers 16, 17
transverse waves 35, 49
treatment of cancer 84
trivial and obvious 19
turbines 17, 63
turns 12, 13, 14, 16
TV and radio waves 42
twilight zone 54
twinkle twinkle 58
twisting 29
types of energy 64

U

ultrasound 47
ultraviolet light 44
units = kW × hours 19
units of electricity 36
"units" of Energy 19
Universe 56, 57
unstable nuclei 82
uranium 81, 83
Uranus 51, 52
UV rays 44

V

V-I graphs 4
vacuum 42, 45, 68
vacuum flask 69, 70
variable resistor 4
velocity 21
Venus 51, 52
vibration energy (heat) 66
vibrations 35, 46, 47
visible light 44
voltage 4, 6, 8, 10, 16, 17
voltmeter 4, 6
volts 4
volume change in gases 33

W

waste energy, heat 16, 71
watts 74
wave equation 36
wave power 63
wavelength 35, 36, 41, 42
waves 35
weight 22, 25, 27
white dwarf 58
wind power/turbines 62
winds 60
wires 4
work done 74

X

X-rays 44

Y

you are here 56

Z

zzzzzzzzzzz 21